JUDGMENT
A CASE OF MEDICAL MALPRACTICE

JUDGMENT
A CASE OF MEDICAL MALPRACTICE

Gail Kessler

ASBURY PARK PUBLIC LIBRARY
ASBURY PARK, NEW JERSEY

MASON/CHARTER

NEW YORK 1976

COPYRIGHT © Gail Kessler 1976

All rights reserved

No part of this book may be reproduced in any form without permission in writing from the publisher

1 2 3 4 5 6 7 8 9 10

Library of Congress Cataloging in Publication Data

Kessler, Gail.
  Judgment : a case of medical malpractice.

  1. Burke, Betty. 2. Malpractice—United States.
I. Title.
KF228.B87K4   346'.73'033   76-25802
ISBN 0-88405-371-7

To Harriet,
for the pieces that fell off the table

ON A HUGE HILL,
CRAGGED, AND STEEP, TRUTH STANDS, AND HE THAT WILL
REACH HER, ABOUT MUST, AND ABOUT MUST GO . . .

—John Donne

AUTHOR'S NOTE

I have made every attempt to tell this true story accurately and without bias.

A few very minor changes have been made in the trial transcripts, hospital records, letters and other documents, only for the sake of clarity.

The names Lou Halprin and Drs. Hellerstein, Van Houten, Rabin, Silverman and Partridge are false; they were changed by request.

Thanks are due to plaintiff's attorney Haskell Shapiro, who provided me with the entire contents of his massive file on the Betty Burke case, and spent many hours explaining various aspects of it to me; to plaintiff's attorney David Sabih; defense attorney Harold Hunter; to jurors Bob Siemann, Kathy Spellman, Emma Oaks, Dolores Loya, Verla Holloway, Roseann Halte and Pete Crosetto for allowing me to interview them, and to Pete Crosetto for sharing with me his copious notes on the case; and especially to Betty Burke, a courageous woman who talked to me frankly and at length about her experiences.

The plaintiff, the attorneys and the jurors were all interviewed in the autumn of 1974.

JUDGMENT
A CASE OF MEDICAL MALPRACTICE

PART ONE

1.

STUDEBAKER HOSPITAL, NORWALK, CALIFORNIA.
APRIL 10, 1967, 2 P.M.

The doctor enters the operating room, gowned and gloved. The patient has been prepared for surgery. She lies face down on the operating table, her red hair almost entirely covered by a sterile cap, an area of her lower back exposed.

The doctor is in his sixties. He has done this operation many times. It holds no surprises for him. He makes the incision, performs the laminectomy, removes the ruptured disk material.

Suddenly his hand slips. He has made a tiny nick in the dura, the sheath that protects the nerves of the spinal cord. Spinal fluid begins to ooze out.

The doctor thinks for a moment. He knows no one of those present will say anything about what has occurred. The leak is minimal; he decides the opening is not large enough to need sutures. He calls for a patch of Surgicel, a cellulose material generally used to stop bleeding, and places it over the leak. In a few seconds it is soaked with fluid, but he is confident the leak will stop shortly and the Surgicel will be absorbed by the body, as always.

He closes the wound. He relaxes. He is tired, and thankful that he is to leave in a few days for a well-earned vacation in Palm Springs.

Did it happen this way?

3

2.

The red-haired woman is driving in the right-hand lane of the Freeway in her Volkswagen. Her seventeen-year-old step-daughter sits beside her. The girl has been visiting for the week-end, and now the woman is taking her back to her home in Huntington Beach.

"Do you think Dad'll be out soon?" the girl asks.

"I think so, honey. I hope so. They said he's doing real well."

Suddenly the engine sputters.

"Damn! Must be out of gas." Stupid to have bought this Volks without a gas gauge—quickly she switches over to the reserve tank. But it takes a few seconds for it to catch, and meanwhile the car is slowing down. "Dammit, come on!"

There is a screeching of brakes, a sickening crash and jolt as the car is hit from behind, shoved several yards forward and comes to an abrupt stop. The two women are slammed back and forth by the impact, banging their heads and knees. They are momentarily stunned. Then the red-haired woman collects her-self as she realizes she is alive and not bleeding anywhere. Her knee hurts. She turns anxiously to her stepdaughter. "You all right, Cherrie?"

The girl nods. "I think so." She manages a nervous laugh.

Shaking a little, the woman gets out of the car to face the other driver. He does not have a car, she sees, but a small pick-up truck with a camper on it. The man comes toward her, white-faced.

"Lady, you could'na been going more'n five miles an hour! You can't do that on a freeway—you coulda got killed!"

4

"You were too close to me!" she retorts. "I didn't slow down more than a tiny bit! You're supposed to be in control of your vehicle!" She knows one is not supposed to admit anything at the scene of an accident. "Look," she says, more quietly, "I don't think I'm hurt. We're both okay. I just want to get my car fixed. The back fender's smashed." They exchange names, phone numbers, insurance information. Traffic has slowed almost to a standstill as rubbernecking drivers gape at the scene.

The Volkswagen will not start. But then the driver of the pick-up truck helps, and finally they manage to get it going. The woman drives off the Freeway at the first off-ramp and calls the Highway Patrol to report the accident.

When she finally gets home, she notices that her right leg is quite swollen. She remembers her knee hitting the dashboard.

The next day her back aches severely, and she tries to take it easy. But she isn't worried. She's been getting on pretty well for a long time, considering what she's been through. She does stumble sometimes, her leg seems to buckle under her—but so what? She's been able to care for her family, do her housework, drive. . . . Sometimes she has pain, but nothing unbearable. Anyway, they'd told her she'd just have to learn to live with it.

There is a phone call. It's Flora Hoover, the elderly nurse who took care of her two years ago when she had all those problems, and who still keeps in touch. Flora has been visiting a friend in the neighborhood, and she says she will drop by later.

When Flora arrives, she becomes visibly upset to see that the red-haired woman is lying down and in pain. "What happened to you?"

"Oh, I was in a little car accident yesterday. Guy hit me from the rear. Banged up my knee, but nothing serious."

Flora frowns, leans over and examines the knee. "Does anything else hurt you? How about your back? Be careful how you move—"

"What on earth's the matter? I'm okay, it's nothing! Look,

if the swelling doesn't go down I'll see the doctor, all right?"
Why does Flora seem so worried? "Flora? What is it?"

The old woman just shakes her head and bites her lip. "Betty, I want you to go to the emergency room of the hospital and let them take a look at you."

"Sure, tomorrow. I promise. Now how about some coffee?"

"No, not tomorrow. Right now. I'll drive you over."

The red-haired woman looks at the nurse. What is this all about? Maybe Flora thinks the accident did something. . . .

The emergency room doctor looks her over, takes her history. When she mentions that she has had back surgery, he becomes concerned. "Who was your doctor?"

"Dr. McReynolds. Chester McReynolds."

He goes away, comes back. "Dr. McReynolds wants you in the hospital by three o'clock tomorrow."

Now she *is* worried. What is it that everybody else knows and she doesn't?

Gene is still in the Sanitarium, so she makes some phone calls, finds someone to watch the children. She surely won't be away longer than overnight.

Dr. McReynolds comes to see her in the hospital the next day. He is concerned, but cheerful. He wants to keep her under observation for a day or two. Meanwhile, he prescribes traction, heat treatments and muscle relaxants for her back. The swelling in the knee has gone down.

A couple of days later she wakes up and tries to get out of bed to go to the bathroom. She cannot move her right leg. Frightened, she touches it. Below the knee there is no sensation at all.

Dr. McReynolds orders a battery of tests, including a myelogram. "It's the accident," he says. "There's scar tissue in there, and the accident jarred things, pulled on the scar tissue."

She has been in the hospital nearly three weeks when Dr. McReynolds comes into her room one afternoon, his face serious. He takes her hand. "I'm sorry, Betty," he says. "You're going to need another operation."

6

3.

I was born in Johnson City, Tennessee, in 1929. Before I was a year old my parents came to California, and I was brought up in Salinas. Salinas . is a valley south of San Francisco, about seventeen miles from Monterey. It's the produce center of the world—lettuce, celery, carrots, broccoli—but it has a lot of industry now. My childhood was spent with horses and rodeos. I dreamed of owning a ranch of my own when I grew up.

My father was a chronic alcoholic. He was from a very wealthy Tennessee family and was terribly spoiled as a young man. He was a mechanic, one of the best from what I understand. My mother left him when I was four. I know he was mean to her but he was very gentle with me. I remember her packing up in the middle of the night. Of course I didn't understand what was going on. I remember seeing her eyes blackened and I know she was always a good woman.

Later, he drowned.

When I started school we lived north of Salinas in a little section called Santa Rita. I went to a one-room school. I had a very normal childhood, did all the normal things kids do, fought with the other kids, loved 'em. My friends always called me Rusty because of my red hair.

I was very outgoing but very sensitive. I felt compassion for people, was always standing up for the underdog, bringing home hurt animals.

My mother remarried. I didn't know exactly what my mother and stepfather's relationship was and must have resented it. My mother worshipped the ground he walked on.

For some reason my stepfather just didn't like girl kids. But it wasn't because of him that things happened to me. It was in spite of him. He was a verbally cruel man, cruel with the tongue. He had a sadistic mind. But I was strong. My parents were Southern Baptists and I was taught respect for your elders and I still feel that very deeply. I despised him, but I didn't let him influence my thoughts later.

I don't ever remember a kindness or affection from him. Sometimes at mealtime he'd say to me, "What are you doing here?" Actually he couldn't have cared less. He was a teaser in a very sadistic way. A pinch would leave a black-and-blue mark. Everybody was supposed to be tough. Maybe that's why he resented girl children. He said to me, "I don't want you using my name." That hurt me very deeply. When I got older, I wouldn't have used his name if it was the last—

I grew up with thoughts of vengeance, plotting and scheming all the ways I'd do away with him. He wouldn't eat mashed potatoes when I cooked them because I told him I was going to put ground glass in his.

My half brother Everett was born when I was eleven. I don't ever think of him as a half brother. We were exceptionally close. When he came along I was afraid Papa would treat him the same way he treated me, and when I saw he didn't, I was happy. As God is my witness, I never resented the fact that Papa loved him and not me. Sometimes they'd go somewhere as a family, and I'd feel left out. But it didn't leave any deep scars. I'd learned how to fulfill my life. God gave me a true love of people.

My mother was always a good mother. She always saw I was well dressed and taken care of. She just loved my stepfather too much. Her life was totally his, and that's an unhealthy love. All of us want to think we can change our men.

But Papa was a good hard worker. He started with nothing and built a huge trucking business. He was a very good provider. At one time he and my mother built the trucking business into quite a financial empire.

She always made excuses for him. Instead of saying to him, "Well now, she's only a child," she would always say to me, "Well now, you know how he is." I think it made me stronger. It would hurt my feelings and make me mad but it built my character. I became what I was in spite of him.

Blaming things on your childhood is a cop-out.

I was very active in school. I wasn't a brainchild but my grades were a little above average. I did boys' things, was on the boys' baseball team, played football, flew kites, rode a motorcycle. I was never a doll-player. I was scrawny and wore my hair in braids because it was so curly. Some people think curly hair is an asset, but I think it was my cross to bear.

I was very healthy as a child. I always had earaches, and once I had appendicitis and once I broke my arm. But that's all.

I matured late. I had no real interest in boys unless they could ride a horse good or swing a bat well. When I was a junior in high school, my mother took me to a doctor because I hadn't started my periods and my tummy had

8

started to protrude. When I found out what they all thought, I was shattered. Even though I ran around with the wilder bunch, my morals were very high.

When I discovered that boys were different from girls, my grades dropped. I ditched school; I don't know why. Finally I just quit school. I don't know why my mother let me.

She finally left my stepdad and took me and Everett and went back East to her people. I was thrilled she was leaving him. I was about fifteen then and my brother was about four. We stayed with my father's sister—quite wealthy, with servants, maids, the whole jazz. They seemed pretty phony to me. I was never impressed with a bank account. I wish I had more of one now, though.

But Papa came for her and they made it up, and then she and Everett and Papa went off back to California and did their thing. I got very homesick for California, my friends, the life I knew. So I called Mother and begged to come home. I heard Papa in the background, "I don't want that brat here, why don't she stay where she is." But she sent me the money for a ticket home.

I took a job as a waitress and paid room and board at home. I worked very hard and very long hours. I used to hear them arguing at night, Papa saying they'd have been a lot better off if I'd stayed back East. Sometimes he'd forbid me to go somewhere and I'd sneak out the window. Mother could never stand up to him. After a big argument with him I moved out. I was sixteen then.

I got my own apartment and got a job as a switchboard operator and started taking evening classes. After a while I took off and went to El Centro to work in the lettuce. I'd been around there all my life and never worked in a lettuce shed. The men packed it and the women trimmed it. I remember the boss said to me, "You never did this before, did you?" I told him, "If you show me how, I can do it as good or better than anybody else." He said, "If you've got that kind of guts, I'll teach you." If I really set my mind to something, I never felt anything was beyond me. I always felt I could do anything anybody else could do. Anybody can guide their own destiny.

I married a fellow that worked in the lettuce. It was a gypsy kind of life. He was extremely jealous and possessive. We could have no friends, I couldn't speak to anyone.

We were married about three years when I left him and became a cocktail waitress at Palm Springs. I had quite an education there. I found out there was more to some jobs than met the eye. The tips were fantastic, but when I was told what some of my duties were, I had to quit. If I'd known what I know now. . . . I was a damn fool. I don't know what I was saving it for. I turned down some chances. . . . I was stupid. So I went to work at Vegas, had a good life, lots of fun, parties. Then back to Palm Springs and from there to Huntington Park in L. A., still as a cocktail waitress. But I decided I wanted to do more with my life than that. I decided I would get an office job. So every day I got the ads. A steel company wanted a Girl Friday so I went to see what a Girl Friday was. I lied like heck about my background and they hired me. It was to do a small payroll for twelve trucks, bills of lading and things. It was the first time I'd seen a ten-key adding machine in action, and I thought, if I don't learn right now I never will. So I watched another woman using one, and I taught myself.

I continued in office work, continued to better myself. I went to East L. A. State College in bookkeeping and various courses. I'd try anything in the office; if somebody was gone I'd always fill in. In each company I went as far as I could go, and if I saw there was no future I'd look around for something better. And one thing I learned was that one way to keep a good job was not to sleep with the boss.

I finally worked myself up to where I was payroll supervisor and personnel manager over a chain of nineteen markets. I'd gotten to know payroll inside and out, and that ten-key monster I could operate as well or better than anybody.

Somewhere along in there I got married again, a fellow I knew up in Salinas. He was the exact opposite of my first husband—fun-loving, a good dancer, real party boy. But he was totally irresponsible, always taking off here and there. I wanted more security. So we separated.

My brother in the meantime had broken up his marriage and gone into the Navy. I'd have more fun going out with him—just raising hell everywhere. With a brother you can do what you want and yet you've got that little bit of security. We used to really have a ball. He'd chase anything with a skirt. Then he'd hit my apartment about an hour before shiptime, and I'd have to get him down there and then get back and get to work. But he was always there when I needed him. We never lost that closeness.

In my first marriage, I wanted children very badly and so did he, and I had many, many pregnancies and miscarriages. They would operate and take out what they had to, and I'd try again. I had one stillborn, I had a tubal pregnancy—I had an ovary the size of a lemon. They eventually found out that the problem was somewhere on the back side of my womb. So finally they had to take everything. And I never really knew what it was, a malfunction or infection. . . . Had they known what the problem was, maybe. . . . I was very hurt.

I had another marriage after I divorced Ray. I can't even remember his name. I didn't love him the way I should. But everything was the way you think it should be when you're young—beautiful wedding and all, and I'd never had a big wedding—I think that was the whole bit. And for a man, he was so naive, maybe that was what attracted me. He didn't believe in sex till after marriage. I don't ever recommend that. My morals were never loose —I was no angel but I just kept one at a time. But I should've known there was something wrong. We were as incompatible—I'm not sure but what I was the first piece of . . . first piece he'd ever had. Good-looking sucker, too, he looked like Kirk Douglas.

So one day he went to work, I stayed home, packed, and by five o'clock I'd moved out, found an apartment and gotten an attorney. I have weekends I can remember better than that marriage. Lots of 'em.

For a while I dated a sheriff's officer. I would work with him on special assignments when they wanted someone who wasn't a known policewoman. I got interested in it, especially in the narcotics part of it. But I had too much compassion. I was putting in 18 or 24 hours at a time. Those young kids in trouble—kids nine years old fixing!—I was bringing them home and getting involved.

I was taking my tests so I could officially go into the detective bureau in narcotics—this was when they were first accepting women—when I met Gene. I was in my late twenties then. Age don't really bother me, but yes, I'm vain, because I think all women should be. . . .

Well, we had an immediate thing going. Gene was very good-looking and he had the qualities I was ready for, that I wanted in a man. And there was the family bit; he had three children and was getting a divorce. Things developed rapidly. I had to quit my assignments, but I don't blame him. What man wants his wife working nights out on the streets with a couple of good-looking cops?

Gene wanted me to meet his children. They were very responsive to me. So that summer he got the children away from their mother and we went up to live in San Jose, and from that time on I've had them. Mitch was just a baby then, Larry was four, and Cherrie was eight. It was beautiful. I was meant to raise those children; God made it possible. I believe in God, I feel

11

very deeply about it. But our minds are not meant to be able to grasp the fullness of it. And we aren't ready to know the future. I wouldn't want to, anyway. Only if I'm going to make it or something.

Gene was very sentimental. He kept saying, "I really think we ought to get married," and I said, "Why knock a good thing? When you get married your troubles start." But the day his divorce was final we drove to Vegas and got married.

Gene had been an illegitimate child, and it preyed on his mind. I didn't read the signs of an alcoholic in Gene but his drinking gradually built and built and built. I hadn't realized his problem was as bad as it was. We separated in 1964. I packed up the boys—Cherrie was with her mother— and went to Salinas. My brother came up, he was between wives. When anything really important's happened in my life, he's always been there. When Gene cut his wrists Everett was in Texas and he took a plane home. He had a Western band at the time and he'd give me his part of the tips to get things I needed for the kids, and he'd bring leftover food.

I went back with Gene. His being an alcoholic, cutting his wrists, didn't have anything to do with my problems. It was all prior.

We bought a house in San Clemente in 1966. It was my first real home of my own. Gene's credit was so bad that we had to struggle to get it. He thought we'd lose the house in six months; he didn't think we could hack it. I was trying to get the house organized and that was why I was moving that bookcase. It was a sectional bookcase, and I took the top rail off, took the books out, and laid them on the bed. Then you lift off the next one, only you have to empty it first. It was on casters, and it started to slide forward. So I grabbed hold of it to try and keep it from falling, and it just kind of brought me to the floor. I thought I had just pulled a muscle. So I lay down for a while, then got up and did a few more things. But it was pretty bad. The next morning I couldn't get out of bed.

The neighbors gave us the name of a doctor, who told me to see this orthopedist. This guy did nothing but poke around on me, give me pain pills, and he told me I had to go to him three times a week in order to draw my disability. Now I knew better, and I told him I wanted a shot of something, I couldn't continue with this pain. He said, "I can't give you a shot and let you drive home."

I said, "You let me be the judge of that. That's not your responsibility." I asked him what he thought it was.

12

He said, "You can't afford to go into the hospital; otherwise I could give you a myelogram." I think that was the first time I ever heard the term myelogram.

I said, "Who are you to judge what I can afford? I have very adequate insurance. If I need some tests, give them to me."

So finally the State Disability sent me a letter to go and be examined by one of their doctors. He examined me very thoroughly—the State pays for that—and the next morning, March 9th, 1967, he put me in the hospital and gave me a myelogram. He told me there were certain parts of your back you couldn't tell were injured or not without this particular kind of test. They put this dye in your back, Pantopaque they call it, with a needle, and it shows up on the x-ray. This was when I found out I had a ruptured disk. He told me I would have to have surgery.

I was terrified at the thought of anyone doing anything to my back. I called our family doctor and he recommended Dr. McReynolds. McReynolds told me to be in Downey at Studebaker Hospital on April 2nd. He put me in a three-bed ward where the other two women were dying. When he came in to get my medical history I told him I wanted just two things—out of that room and something for pain. And I'm very much against narcotics. My system needs twice as much of anything to even affect me. If I wanted to get hooked I'd have to start with a $60-a-day habit. Anyway, within fifteen minutes he had me moved to a two-bed room.

He seemed to be very competent. He said not to be afraid, disks are removed all the time and people survive nicely. I'd heard these old wives' tales about what happens to backs. . . . I had mixed emotions about Dr. McReynolds. I still do.

At this point he still hadn't seen the x-rays. It was merely my word that I had a ruptured disk. The night prior to the surgery I was beginning to get a little nervous, and I said, "What do you do, do you give me another myelogram?"

He said, "No, I'll look at the x-rays from that one."

I said, "You mean you're going to operate on me and you haven't even seen the x-rays?" I was about to hit Panicsville. I called my husband, and he drove down to the hospital at 9:30 at night and had to go through all kinds of red tape to have the x-rays released to him. Dr. McReynolds waited at the hospital for them. And I went to surgery the next afternoon at 2 P.M.

13

Testimony of Dr. McReynolds, October 2, 1973:
"She insisted, and the family insisted, that the myelogram showed a ruptured disk. But I assured them I wasn't going to operate on her back without having seen the myelogram films. And so I believe her husband brought them in."

4.

STUDEBAKER HOSPITAL, NORWALK, CALIFORNIA.
APRIL 10, 1967. 2 P.M.

Operation Record
Procedure: With the patient under general anesthesia, lying prone on the operating table, with the hips slightly flexed, the lumbosacral spine was exposed by an incision in the midline from L3 to the sacrum. The muscles were reflected on the right side to expose the lamina of L4 and L5 and sacrum . . . A laminectomy was performed on the lower portion of the lamina of L4 to visualize the L4-L5 disk. . . . The disk surface was bulging moderately and was somewhat soft. The nerve root was pinched between the bulging disk and the dorsal structures. The nerve root was retracted, the disk was entered and a large amount of soft disk material removed. The nerve root canals were probed and the nerve roots were found to lie entirely free in their canals.

The operative field was inspected. There was no bleeding. A #20 gauge needle was inserted through the dural sac and probably 2–3 cc. of Pantopaque dye was aspirated. This was further explored by tilting the patient with her hips down and her torso tilted upward. By tilting her toward the right side, it was felt that most of the Pantopaque remaining in the dural sac was removed. There was very minimal leak of spinal fluid. A small patch of Surgicel was placed over the defect and the wound was closed. . . . Telfa and dry gauze dressing applied.

Immediate post-operative condition good.

Estimated blood loss less than 300 cc. There was no need felt to replace it with a transfusion.

C. C. McReynolds, M.D.

The wound is closed. The object on the table again becomes a human being, a red-haired woman named Betty Burke. She is wheeled away to the recovery room.

The surgeon relaxes. He is tired, and thankful that he is to leave in a few days for a well-earned vacation in Palm Springs.

Did it happen this way?

It was six years before Betty Burke saw this report, but it might as well have been in Sanskrit; it was incomprehensible to her at first. So she did a little research in an anatomy book.

She learned that the vertebrae of the spine are divided into the cervical (upper), the thoracic (middle), the lumbar (lower) and the sacral (lowest). Each of the vertebrae is given an initial (C for cervical, T for thoracic, L for lumbar, S for sacral) and a number: the fourth and fifth lumbar vertebrae, for instance, are known as L4 and L5. Between the bodies of the vertebrae are the disks, which connect and cushion the vertebrae, serving as shock absorbers. They are composed of a nucleus of soft, pulpy, elastic material, and a rim of fibrous tissue. Sometimes the disk becomes herniated, or "slipped," which means that the hard outer rim is ruptured, and the nucleus extrudes. It sounded something like a jelly doughnut, Betty thought. If the doughnut is squeezed too hard, its outer rim breaks and the jelly oozes out.

This type of injury, she learned, occurs most often between the L4 and L5 vertebrae, because this is the area that bears the most weight in our activities. This was where her own herniated disk had occurred.

The lamina is the back (or dorsal) part of the vertebra, the bony structure that can be felt by running the hand along the spine. In order to get at the disk, the surgeon must remove part of this bone in an operation called a laminectomy.

The dural sac, she read, is the canal that encloses the nerves of the spinal cord. This canal passes through the openings in the centers of the vertebrae, and is protected in back by the dorsal structures, and in front by the bodies of the vertebrae. When a disk is herniated or ruptured, the protruding disk material can press on the nerves, injuring them and causing pain.

5.

When Betty Burke came to after surgery, she noticed that there was a nurse in constant attendance upon her. She'd had other operations in her life—an appendectomy when she was a child, a hysterectomy in her early twenties—and this seemed unusual to her. Why did she need a private nurse?

"Because the doctor ordered it, dear. How do you feel?"

"Okay. My leg feels kinda numb, that's all. What's your name?"

"Flora. Flora Hoover."

Later, Dr. McReynolds came to see his patient. He pronounced her in fine condition, had her move her ankles and toes and knees and nodded his head approvingly. "You'll be up and around in a couple of weeks. Now, there was nothing to be so frightened of, was there?"

Betty smiled. She liked this man. He was so fatherly you couldn't help having confidence in him.

On the 14th of April, Betty felt well, apart from the problem of gas that one generally has after an operation. Dr. McReynolds wrote in his daily report that she was making good progress, was cheerful and comfortable, had no back pain, and was moving her toes, feet, ankles and knees well. The "numbness" in her leg had subsided. She had reported some feeling of "pressure" in the coccygeal area, but he did not consider it significant, and left for his vacation.

On April 24th, the sutures were taken out by a Dr. Mooney in the absence of Dr. McReynolds. Mooney expressed some yellow fluid from the wound. The patient had been complaining for several days of pain and pressure in the tailbone area ("like someone kicked me real hard," she said) and of a persistent headache. And she had never been a headache-prone person, she said. Her neck seemed stiff, too; it was difficult to turn her head.

That night Betty awoke to find her sheets soaked.

Can I have wet the bed? she thought. That didn't seem possible. Besides, it was in the wrong place—under her back. Blood? Frightened, she switched on the light and called to the nurse. No, it was not blood, it was water, or a watery fluid. The nurse told her not to worry, and changed the sheets.

When Dr. Mooney came the next day she told him about the sheets being wet. He didn't seem particularly concerned. He examined her back. "Dr. McReynolds isn't around just now," he said. "We'll wait until he comes back. I'm sure it's nothing serious. Probably a little abscess."

It happened again. This time the sheets had to be changed twice during the night, and again during the day. The headaches seemed to be getting worse. Two other doctors came in and examined Betty. "We'd better have McReynolds take a look at this," they said.

"Well, where is Dr. McReynolds?" Betty demanded.

"On vacation. He'll be back in a day or two."

"He'd better be."

Dr. McReynolds came back on the 26th. He observed a small lump at the site of the incision. "It's just a little abscess," he told Betty. "It happens sometimes after surgery. We'll get that fluid out this afternoon."

When he went away Betty began to cry a little. Mrs. Hoover, the day nurse, came over to her. "What's the matter? Not feeling well? Does it hurt?"

"Yes, it hurts. But it's not just that, it's—well, I thought everything was all right, that it was all over. Now he says I have an abscess."

"Don't you worry that red head of yours one bit. Dr. McReynolds will take care of that for you, and you're going to be just fine."

When Dr. McReynolds inserted the needle in Betty's back she thought she heard someone screaming. Then she realized it was she herself. It felt as if her head were being blown off, she said later. Afterward she had to lie very still and remain on her right side.

The next day her head still hurt, her back hurt, and she was terribly discouraged. Dr. McReynolds had told her she would improve when he took the fluid out. But when the nurse tried to comfort her, she refused to talk about it. What was the good of talking?

On the 28th, Gene visited. He tried to come every day, but he couldn't always make it. Betty looked forward to visiting hour, as all the patients did. It was the high point of the day. She felt a little better.

But after sitting up for supper that evening, her head suddenly began to hurt terribly. Her tongue felt thick and dry, and both her legs ached. She told the nurse, who called Dr. Mooney. He removed the binder Betty had been wearing, and the dressing. The abscess seemed to be filling up again, he said. He would inform Dr. McReynolds.

All the next day Betty was restless and apprehensive. When was Dr. McReynolds going to come? She was given Demerol and Seconal and several other kinds of medication, even more than usual, but they were not sufficient to kill the pain and relax her. Dr. McReynolds came in the late afternoon and again aspirated fluid from her back. Again, it was agonizing.

But the pain in Betty's head and back and legs did not go away. On the afternoon of May 1st, Dr. McReynolds came in to talk to her. She had a little cyst on her back, he said, and cleaning it out had not solved the problem. It was unfortunate, but these things sometimes happened after surgery. She would have to have a second operation to remove the cyst.

Betty cried. It was beginning to seem as though this would never end.

McReynolds patted her hand. "It's a very, very minor thing," he said. "Won't take more than a couple of stitches. Nothing to be upset about." He paused. "Are you concerned

18

about the money, Betty? It'll only be half price this time. A bargain." He smiled at her. She tried to smile back. That was thoughtful of him.

6.

STUDEBAKER HOSPITAL, NORWALK, CALIFORNIA.
MAY 2, 1967. 2:05 P.M.

Operation Record
Procedure: With the patient lying prone, the previous operative scar was opened. The fluid-filled cavity under the fascia was emptied. . . . After the fluid was aspirated, the defect in the dura was immediately evident. This was closed using four interrupted 5–0 black silk sutures. There was no demonstrable leak from this repair. The wound was then freed of its layer of scar lining the cavity in the deep muscle layer. . . . The subcutaneous cystic area was stripped of its layer of scar. . . . The skin was closed. Telfa and dry gauze dressing applied. Immediate post-operative condition good.

C. C. McReynolds, M. D.

7.

NORWALK SUPERIOR COURT.
OCTOBER 16, 1973.

Q. Can you just very briefly tell us about your condition for the balance of 1967? That is, after May 2nd?
A. Well, for a while I had to stay in bed. Then I improved and I was walking. And the pain persisted, but it

19

did diminish somewhat for a little while and then it increased. I can't really remember in detail at what point it increased, or describe exactly what kind of pain, because too much has happened to me since.

Q. Of course. But generally speaking, you were able to walk?

A. Oh, yes.

Q. All right. Then you would get prescriptions from Dr. McReynolds to relieve you of pain?

A. Oh, yes, and sometimes muscle relaxants.

Q. How about 1968 and 1969, did you go and see Dr. McReynolds?

A. Yes.

Q. You were able to walk?

A. Yes.

Q. Was there any weakness in your legs or were you—

A. In my right leg.

Q. Did you have pains or any critical problems—excuse me, Betty, are you uncomfortable now?

A. No, I just need to shift a little bit once in a while. Yes—they were pains that—well, I had been told I would have to live with. I did my daily functions, but I would have to rest and lay down in between times.

Q. Were your legs very strong or did you have some weakness there?

A. The right leg, I had weakness. I had to cater to it because it was painful. It's hard to explain. It was like kind of electricity going down your leg. Putting weight or anything on it was painful.

8.

Post-operative record. C. C. McReynolds, M.D.

August 4, 1967. No pain pills in weeks now. Walking freely. Up A.M. and housework and shopping. Lie down rest 1½ hours P.M.—up all late afternoon. Rest in evenings. Bed 11 P.M.—8 A.M. Sleeps normally. Not awakened at night by back unless she goes to sleep supine.

September 1, 1967. Patient has moderately severe tenderness right side para-median incision area. Wears "that brace" with binder more or less. Pain awakens and keeps patient awake past 3 nights. Pain radiation to low right buttock produced by lifting leg from weight bearing in gait. Was fine until past one week.

September 15, 1967. Soma compound helped the first week. Tenderness right lumbosacral junction, pain with walking sometimes. Headaches, top left side recurrent.

September 25, 1967. Says wearing brace does not ease pain, makes her more uncomfortable. Went fishing for 1½ hours on pier Saturday without binder or brace, severe low back pain relieved by taking medications and lying down. Doing better, muscles right lower extremity sore "all the time" from straining.

October 9, 1967. The patient did not keep her appointment.

October 19, 1967. Patient is comfortable in brace over binder for riding and driving. Gets up to get children off to school and husband to work, maximum time up two hours before she gets muscle spasm right back and upper lumbar to right buttock. Over that time has to rest on reclining chair. Soma compound 3–5 times a day, none some days. Severe muscle spasm relieved best with Norflex 1, sometimes 2, at 4 hours. Given a prescription for Winstrol 2 mgm.

November 16, 1967. The patient did not keep her appointment.

December 28, 1967. The patient did not keep her appointment.

May 27, 1968. Patient stands better than she can sit. Pain right buttock, knee and anterior shin. Straight leg raising to 65/80 degrees, numbness in right foot all the time. Remitting episodes of complete numbness right lower extremity, buttock, thigh and leg including foot for 7–10 minutes, gradually return. Two episodes loss of active motion, entire lower extremity: once before falling one month ago, and once since. Tailbone hurts right side. Sharp sudden "shower" of headaches right vertex lasting a few minutes. Prescribed Dilantin 100 mgm daily.

April 1, 1969. The patient did not keep her appointment.

August 11, 1969. Patient admitted to Studebaker Hospital for traction following automobile accident.

August 27, 1969. Lumbar myelogram.

August 30, 1969. Surgery. Surgeon Dr. Spindle, assistant surgeon Dr. McReynolds.

9.

At this point he brought in Spindle. Spindle walks in the night before surgery and says, "I'm Fat Jesus." He had a pointed black beard. He didn't say it with any smile or anything, I think he really thought he was. That's the only name I knew him by for about three days.

He says, "I'm the doctor doing the surgery tomorrow. How are you going to pay for it?"

I said, "It will be paid for."

He says, "How?"

I said, "You're serious, aren't you?"

He says, "What do you think I'm in the business for?"

I told him that frankly I didn't really know how it would be paid for, because my husband was in the Sanitarium. I didn't know if our insurance would cover it.

10.

STUDEBAKER HOSPITAL, NORWALK, CALIFORNIA.
AUGUST 30, 1969. 9 A.M.

Operation Record
Procedure: Routine prepping and draping of the back was carried out. Previous scar was opened. The muscles were reflected. The lumbosacral space was identified and more bone was taken off. The scar tissue was stripped with a 15 blade. I then retracted the dural sac and saw there was still some bulging disk. The disk was removed, both right and left sides. I then opened the dura at the lumbosacral space. It was markedly thickened and I could see a tangled nerve rootlet. I did a laminectomy at the next space and came from good dura downwards where I could then open up and see the escape of spinal fluid. I picked up each nerve root with a nerve hook and gently stripped it downward, removing the adhesions. At places the nerve rootlets were completely plastered to the inside of the dura by arachnoidal adhesions. I then put in 40 mgs. of Depo Medrol and closed the dura. . . . Prognosis immediate and remote will have to be somewhat guarded as it is problematical how these

23

patients do after massive surgery. However, the long term outlook may well be favorable.

David Spindle, M.D.

11.

When I woke up from that surgery I felt like I had a huge strop or something between my legs. And it was the numbness. So in just a short time I was paralyzed on the right side. By November of the following year I was almost totally paralyzed. They said I needed another operation for scar tissue.

I kept explaining to Dr. Spindle that the only way my bowels could move was that when it came down so I could feel it, I would take it out. He said, "That'll be all right, it'll come around." The next time I went, I was describing it in detail, because it was bothering me. So he said I was neurotic. He wrote to McReynolds saying that I was becoming neurotic by describing my bowels in detail. I had never thought of myself as being neurotic. I asked Dr. McReynolds if I was. He said no. He knew I didn't like Spindle. He said, "It's like taking a car to a garage. You don't have to like the mechanic if he's good." That made sense.

November 20, 1969.
Dear Dr. McReynolds:

Mrs. Burke comes in today complaining of constipation. She says she has a stool every morning of "perfectly round balls" and emphasizes that the balls are perfect.

I gave her a bowel training type of program. She states that her vagina is completely numb from the lips inward, and this "plays hell with sexual intercourse."

Of her previous paralysis, only that of the foot is left; and she is able to walk and dance. On the whole, I think she is somewhat of a success story. I think she probably does indeed have some problem with defecation because of interference of the lower sacral segments; however, it is my feeling she probably will be able to return to sexual satisfaction.

I gave her some counsel in this regard, but she seemed to reject it, stating she had been a psychology major in school. In addition to her problem, I feel she has extreme psychoneurotic tendencies.

Yours very truly,
David Spindle, M.D.

12.

Q. Dr. Spindle, could you tell us what your findings were when you examined Betty before her fourth operation in December, 1970?

A. At that time . . . Betty was really bad. She was almost a basket case, I thought. Excuse me if I'm using the wrong terminology. I don't mean to offend anybody, but Betty was in bad shape and Dr. McReynolds had asked me to see her, and I . . . really didn't want to see her again because I was afraid that—well, usually arachnoiditis is a one-shot deal and you don't want to go in and operate the second time, very frankly. When I saw her I found her to be walking but she had had a loss of sphincter control. She had intense numbness.

She had vaginal numbness, rectal numbness and marked weakness of the right leg, and I felt that she was at least as bad, if not worse, than when I had seen her prior to the last surgery.

Q. Isn't it true that you did not want to do another operation on her in December of 1970?

A. That is correct.

Q. Was it at the urging of Dr. McReynolds that you consented to do another one?

A. Dr. McReynolds is a very empathetic physician. So with gentle persuasion I did indeed see her, and spent a

25

great deal of time talking to Betty about the possible dismal results of any further surgery, but she felt that she had been helped by the previous surgery, and we felt we would have another go at it.

Q. Doctor . . . were you not afraid that the result could be total and complete paralysis of the lower extremities?

A. I felt that that was a definite possibility and instructed the patient that she could have total permanent paralysis of her lower extremities.

Q. Did you tell her that she might forever lose control of her bowels?

A. I believe she had already lost control of them. I have already testified elsewhere that I felt that she would eventually end up as a paraplegic.

Q. Will you describe the operation that you performed on her on December 11th, 1970.

A. This time instead of finding just arachnoiditis, I found intradural metaplastic bone. She actually had bone growing in the dural canal, with nerve roots going through it. The adhesions were dense. Even under magnification I couldn't tell what was scar and what was nerve root. I stimulated the nerve to see whether there was any functional neural tissue. I did a tedious dissection, dissected out these pieces of bone in between these tangled horses' tails of nerve root and removed them, tediously testing each little strand to see if it was functioning neural tissue.

I realized now that I had to do something different than I did in the prior operation. I used a material called Silastic, which is a completely inert material, marketed as dural substitute. I use it all the time, as neurosurgeons do, and it causes no tissue reaction. I made a tube that went above the arachnoiditis to below it, hoping that this might convey some spinal fluid, and by bathing the nerves in spinal fluid might be of some benefit to Betty.

That is what I did and she got up and she walked. She got up and walked and cooked dinner, she told me, I think, for 20 or 23 people on Easter.

26

Q. That improvement though was unfortunately short-lived; is that correct?

A. You are right. Unfortunately it was short-lived.

13.

The insurance company representing Thomas Kuykendall, the driver of the pick-up truck that hit Betty Burke's Volkswagen, offered Betty $6000 after her third operation, performed by Dr. Spindle in August, 1969. This was a ridiculously low amount, she thought, considering all she had been through. She decided she needed a lawyer.

Her mother happened to know a Los Angeles lawyer named Haskell Shapiro. Betty telephoned him from the hospital. He came to see her, and after hearing her story, advised her to bring suit. She retained him to represent her. They were going to ask for $25,000, the limit of Kuykendall's insurance policy.

Haskell Shapiro was a self-made man, a living embodiment of the American Dream. The youngest of a family of four children, he had been three years old when his father died in the influenza epidemic of 1918. Haskell's mother went to work as a saleswoman in a cosmetics shop in Brooklyn, New York, and the children had to learn to take care of themselves. Haskell was extremely bright; he skipped several grades in elementary school and began high school at eleven. When he graduated, he and his mother moved to Los Angeles to be near his married sister, and he entered a pre-med course at U. S. C.

At fifteen, in addition to being the youngest student in the University and unable to compete with his classmates either physically or socially, he had a severe stutter, which persisted into his twenties. Whenever he stammered, he would blush, and the blushing persisted long after the stutter was gone.

At sixteen, restless, Haskell hitchhiked to New York,

where he worked at odd jobs and attended C.C.N.Y. During the next few years he moved back and forth from coast to coast several times. In 1935, at twenty, he went again to California, expecting this time to continue on to China or wherever the wind blew him. But instead he got married, lost some of his restlessness, and stopped stuttering.

He worked as a truck driver for the ice cream division of Thrifty Drugs in Los Angeles, and went to school at night—first in civil engineering, then accounting, then education. But nothing satisfied him.

During the war, he took a second full-time job, as a filter operator at Birely's, a maker of non-carbonated beverages, and temporarily stopped school. Each was a 7-day, 56-hour job. He worked the day shift at Thrifty, and the "graveyard" shift at Birely's. When he had the chance, he volunteered for the "swing" or in-between shift at Birely's as well, so that he was working twenty-four hours a day. In addition, he often volunteered to deliver ice cream to the Air Force Base in Riverside. He would start the Birely's job at midnight, work hard and fast and get all his work done by 3 A.M. Then he would run over to Thrifty, drive to Riverside and return by 5:30 (having picked up a few cases of eggs from the farms on his route, which—eggs being scarce at that time—he would sell to the men on the incoming shift at Birely's). He would then return to Birely's and finish his shift there at 8 A.M., when he started the day at Thrifty. He caught a few hours of sleep now and then when he could.

Often, the total number of hours on Haskell's combined paychecks came to well over the total numbers of hours in a week.

In 1949, he entered law school, going nights and working only one 60-hour job. He passed the bar with no difficulty in 1953, by which time he and his wife had four children.

When Betty Burke retained him, he was in his middle fifties, a wealthy and successful attorney, still working and playing as hard as three or four normal men, sleeping practically not at all, and enjoying life enormously. Most of his practice

28

was in personal injury cases, so Betty Burke's auto accident case held nothing unusual for him. He did not dream, when he agreed to represent her, that his connection with Betty would eventually bring him the biggest case of his career.

14.

By July of 1971, when the case came to trial, Betty had undergone her fourth operation. After the third and fourth operations there had been marked improvement, lasting a few months in each case, and then gradual deterioration. After the fourth operation, particularly, she had made such a dramatic recovery that Dr. Spindle felt justified in calling her "a success story." That was in December, 1970. But around the middle of March her sensory and motor powers began to decrease noticeably.

Dr. McReynolds examined her in his office on June 7, 1971, at Haskell Shapiro's request. He reported that Betty's walking capacity was minimal, that she was in constant pain, was so constipated that she had to remove fecal matter by hand, and could only urinate by applying hand pressure to her bladder. Her left leg was "dull," her right leg "anesthetic." She had no sensation in the vaginal area. He ended: "Patient is permanently and totally disabled. There is no expectation of any significant function recovery motor or sensory."

Haskell Shapiro had for some time been trying to obtain complete medical reports on Betty from Drs. McReynolds and Spindle, and had found both of them to be very reticent about providing this information, particularly about clarifying the relationship between the auto accident and the need for an operation. He thought this most unusual; doctors ordinarily sent him their reports and bills with no hesitation, knowing that settlement of the case would protect their fees. Finally, shortly before the trial, Dr. McReynolds sent him a brief note:

This patient was able to carry on her care of her family and her home with some help during the fifteen months interval from the time of her last exam here May 27, 1968 until the injury in the traffic accident August, 1969. Since this injury in 1969, she has been totally disabled as previously discussed. This, therefore, historically establishes the fact of total disability as the result of the injury of August, 1969. This is in the nature of an aggravation of a previously existing partial disability, but the present total disability status is now certainly permanent and stationary.

The strongest word Dr. McReynolds would use to support the relationship between the accident and Betty's present condition was "historically."

It seemed to Haskell Shapiro that neither doctor was at all eager to testify at the trial. They didn't think they'd be able to help Betty very much, they said. Dr. Spindle wanted to be assured ahead of time that he would be paid $250 for his testimony.

The doctors were right. They didn't help Betty very much. They admitted, under cross-examination by the defense, that Betty's arachnoiditis—the scar tissue that had formed inside the spinal canal and gradually choked off the nerves—was a condition that takes a very long time to develop. It could not possibly have been the result of the automobile accident. They did insist that the trauma of the accident had aggravated her disorder and contributed to her present condition, but they would not testify to more than that.

Up to that point, Dr. McReynolds had done nothing to correct Betty's impression that her disability was the result of the accident. Wanting to believe this, she testified that for eight or nine months before the accident she had been completely symptom-free. "I was as healthy as you are," she told the defense lawyer. She had gone water surfing, she said, two days before the accident. This testimony was to do her a good deal of harm later.

There was some doubt in the jury's mind as to the extent of Thomas Kuykendall's negligence. Betty Burke claimed to have been going at 45 miles an hour when the accident occurred. But her stepdaughter, Cherrie, faltered badly under cross-examination. "How fast were you going?" She hesitated. "Was it more than five miles an hour?"

"I think so," she replied.

Under California law, any contributory negligence on the plaintiff's part constitutes a complete defense to an act of negligence on the defendant's part. Even if the plaintiff is only one per cent negligent and the defendant 99 per cent so, the plaintiff cannot recover.

Cherrie's hesitation on the stand was fatal to Betty's case. The jury felt that because her Volkswagen was going too slowly, and was an impediment to traffic, the accident was partly her fault. Furthermore, they were convinced that her condition was caused by something other than the accident. They brought in a verdict for the defendant.

Haskell took Betty to lunch after the trial was over. She was stunned. She could not believe that she was to get nothing; for nearly two years she had been looking forward to winning this case. She kept thinking about the money and about all her unpaid medical bills. How she could have used that $25,000!

Betty badly needed something to console her and Haskell decided to tell her what he had been thinking about during the last part of the trial. "Forget that $25,000," he said. "How would you like a million?"

"Who wouldn't? But it'd be kinda hard to rob a bank. I don't get around too well."

"Listen, baby, we've lost a battle, but we haven't lost the war," Haskell said.

"I'm listening."

"We've been suing the wrong people." Betty looked mystified. "Weren't you listening to the last part of McReynolds' testimony? Where he admitted that arachnoiditis takes a long time to develop, a couple of years, maybe?"

"Well, I thought he was just repeating all the things he

31

told me. And I was so tired of listening, I just kind of tuned out."

"I'm convinced that Dr. McReynolds did something wrong, and has been covering it up all these years. Naturally he wanted you to believe that the accident caused your problems. And he convinced you of that, didn't he?"

Betty was silent for several moments. "You mean—I'd have to sue Dr. McReynolds?" she asked. "But I couldn't do that, he's been very good to me, very concerned about me—"

"Of course he's concerned about you; no one says he's not. And he tried to do his best for you. All I'm saying is that I think he made a mistake, a serious mistake, and then to protect his reputation, couldn't admit it. I'm not quite sure yet just what that mistake was. But we'll find out.

"Now, I'm no malpractice expert—I've never handled a medical malpractice case, in fact—but I do know one. Lou Halprin. He was a doctor for twenty-one years, and he's been a lawyer now for ten years, and all he does is malpractice cases."

"What's he like?"

"Well, he's not impressive to look at—kind of short and round—but he's an excellent attorney and a very warm, sincere human being. I have the highest regard for him. You think it over, and if you decide you'd like to talk to him, let me know."

Betty stubbed out her cigarette decisively. "I don't have to think it over. Of course I want to talk to him."

Lou Halprin and Haskell Shapiro drove to San Clemente to see Betty about three weeks after the end of the trial. She was lying in bed, her curly red hair on the white pillow making a dramatic frame for the strong, angular face that had begun to show the lines of pain and stress. She smoked cigarette after cigarette as Halprin questioned her about her operations. He told her he thought she had a good case, and she signed a retainer agreement. Halprin said he would file the complaint and begin looking for experts to testify that there had been negligence.

In December, Haskell flew to Seattle and interviewed Flora

Hoover, the private-duty nurse who had attended Betty after her first and second surgeries. Mrs. Hoover was seventy-two years old, feisty and independent, and proud of having been a registered nurse for forty-eight years. She told Haskell that Dr. McReynolds had instructed her not to discuss with Betty the cause of the spinal fluid cyst that had made a second operation necessary. She was not to indicate to Betty that the leakage of spinal fluid and the cyst had any connection with Betty's first surgery.

Flora Hoover's deposition was taken May 20, 1972. She repeated what she had said about Dr. McReynolds' instructions to her: whenever she asked him a question about the patient, he would remind her not to discuss Betty's condition with her because Betty was "too emotional." Flora did not think Betty was particularly emotional.

Haskell began to wonder why so little progress had been made in the nine months since Lou Halprin had agreed to take the case. Could anything have happened to diminish Lou's enthusiasm for it? Haskell had kept in touch with Betty; he knew she was deeply depressed, in constant pain, and could not walk at all now. He wrote to Halprin:

> I know how busy we both are, but I feel so sorry for our client, Betty Burke, who lies helpless in her wheelchair all day and in pain which is becoming more severe all the time, that I feel we must do whatever is possible to expedite progress on her case.

And Halprin replied:

> In all candor, may I suggest that her condition will not vary irrespective of the outcome of the trial. I am well familiar with what she has; the problem is connecting it with what she had.

Halprin had already had some consultations with doctors, he said. The results had been rather bleak, but he was not discouraged. "I have asked another doctor to look at this for us, and it may be that we may have a better conclusion." He was not being derelict, he insisted. The case required a monumental amount of work and he wanted to approach it systematically.

At the end of August, Halprin sent to Dr. Peter Rabin, a well-known neurosurgeon, a set of facts he had assembled on the Betty Burke case, entitled, "Is It or Is It not a Case?":

"Following a back injury, a myelogram performed on March 9, 1967, allegedly disclosed a ruptured disk at the level of L4-L5. On April 10, 1967, Chester C. McReynolds, M.D., performed a laminectomy and removal of disk material. During the operation, he inserted a 20-gauge needle in the dura and removed 2 to 3 cc. of Pantopaque dye. He then noted 'minimal leakage of spinal fluid' from the opening that he had created with the spinal needle.

"In his judgment this opening did not require suturing, and he therefore applied a patch of Surgicel and after the operation was completed, sewed the patient up.

"Within a week or two he noted swelling in the low back in the region of the incision and shortly thereafter a walnut-size mass in the low back, which he correctly diagnosed as a cerebro-spinal fluid cyst.

"On May 2, 1967, he went in again surgically, aspirated and removed the spinal fluid, removed a connective or scar tissue or fibrous tissue scar which had encapsulated the spinal fluid, and sutured the dural defect through which the cerebro-spinal fluid had leaked into the wound.

"He admitted on deposition that the opening in the dura that he had corrected and closed with four interrupted 5–0 black silk sutures was the same opening that he had created by inserting the 20-gauge needle on April 10 to remove the Pantopaque dye.

"Following a minimal automobile accident on August 7 of 1969, she was again hospitalized, and an exploratory operation performed on August 30, 1969 disclosed extensive arachnoiditis. He admitted that the onset of arachnoiditis or the cause of the arachnoiditis had nothing to do with the automobile acci-

34

dent of some three weeks prior to that surgery.

"The plaintiff-patient is now totally and permanently disabled; she is virtually a paraplegic because of the arachnoiditis.

"It all seems to fall back on to that minimal leakage of spinal fluid that the doctor observed emanating from the dural sac on April 10, 1967, when he applied a patch of Surgicel to that small opening in the dura. Obviously, the Surgicel did not hold, and a cerebro-spinal fluid cyst developed in the low back, connecting with the intrathecal spaces through that same small opening in the dura.

"Question: Did anything that defendant doctor did fall within conduct below the standard of care in the community?"

15.

Dr. Rabin gave his opinion: there was no evidence of negligence or of conduct below the standard of care.

On August 28th Lou Halprin took a deposition from Dr. McReynolds. He wrote to Haskell that McReynolds "told a straight-forward story and made a good impression. I did not think that he answered untruthfully at any time. . . . Thus far my information from consulting physicians is that everything that he did was proper and in fact is what is usually done."

"What we have here," Halprin wrote, "is a case in which certain routine surgeries were followed by catastrophic results without proof of negligence and with allegations that the cause of her terrible condition is not completely understood or known.

"I have yet to find anyone who is willing to say that anything Dr. McReynolds did was below the standard of care in that or in any community. . . . The defense have indicated that they would be willing to pay some minimal settlement."

Haskell shook his head in discouragement as he read the letter. It seemed to him that Lou Halprin had succumbed to the general awe in which surgeons are held by the public.

Thus it seemed to be for the sake of form that Halprin conferred, in April 1973, with another top neurologist, Dr. Hal Gregg. He reported to Haskell:

"Dr. Gregg expressed the opinion that the arachnoiditis resulted from the insertion of the Pantopaque dye into the subarachnoid space. Unfortunately, a small percentage of individuals who undergo myelograms react, for reasons that are not clear, with arachnoiditis. Such reaction may be on an allergic basis.

"Another competent producing cause of arachnoiditis is a blunt injury to the back, and you will remember that she first injured herself when she fell against the bookcase in her home sometime in 1966."

Lou Halprin had arrived at the conclusion that "there is no evidence to support negligence on the part of any doctor. . . .

"I am attempting to obtain some form of settlement on the ground that the carrier might feel that it is better to pay something than to go to trial.

"I think we should inform Betty Burke that I see no hope of winning."

16.

Haskell Shapiro's courage failed him at the thought of breaking this news to Betty. Since she had lost the auto accident case, all that kept her going had been the hope that at long last she might obtain some compensation for the catastrophe that had befallen her. While he was considering the implications of Halprin's decision, Lou telephoned. "I have a little bit of good news," he said. "They're offering us $10,000."

"Well . . . I think that's an absurdly low sum for a shattered life."

36

"Haskell, it's a lot more than nothing. They're under no obligation to give us anything, it's a pure gift, and we owe it entirely to my good relationship with the defense firm. Have you called Betty yet?"

"Not yet."

"Good. This should cheer her up."

"I'm not sure about that, but I'll tell her."

Betty had been receiving therapy at the Orange County Rehabilitation Center for the past several months. For a long time after her last operation, she had not gone to any doctor other than her family one, Dr. Todd. She usually wore slacks, but on one of her visits to him she happened to wear a skirt. Dr. Todd took one look at her atrophied legs and said, horrified, "My God, Rusty, aren't you getting any therapy?"

He immediately signed Betty into the Rehabilitation Center. The x-rays they took there showed that because of her paralysis, and the constipation caused by the constant use of pain-killing drugs, parts of her bowel had stretched completely out of shape. There was talk of doing a colostomy, but Betty refused. She'd rather die than live that way, she said.

They tried first just cleaning me out. That was quite an experience. Because of the pain medication it was all hard as rocks. They were many weeks just getting me cleaned out, and they tried all the systems that have been used on other paraplegics. But because of the shape of my bowels I either didn't react at all or I over-reacted, I would just go all over. Then my wheelchair broke, and they got me one from the ortho floor. But the seat was too long, and my tailbone hit on it, and I developed a decubitus, a sore. I said, "Nobody but me could come to a hospital to get one." Within three days it was a big ulcer. That was my introduction to decubiti.

Haskell called Betty at the hospital and told her of the $10,000 offer, and that Lou recommended taking it.

Betty's immense disappointment and frustration turned to anger. "The only time I've ever seen him was when he signed me up," she said. "If the case is about to be over, don't you think it would be kinda nice if he came to see me and told me what's going on?"

Haskell promised he would arrange the meeting.

Lou Halprin and Haskell drove to the hospital together, a certain tension between them for the first time in their long friendship. They went into the conference room with Betty. His chubby face serious, Halprin explained that all his research and his conferences with the top doctors in the field, as well as the deposition he had taken from Dr. McReynolds, had led him to the inescapable conclusion that there had been no negligence.

"When Dr. McReynolds completed the laminectomy," he told Betty, "he decided to remove the excess Pantopaque dye that had been left in your spinal tract a month earlier, during your myelogram. Rather than being criticized, he ought to be praised for his conscientiousness. Most doctors would have just left it alone.

"He decided to use a 20-gauge needle to remove it. This wasn't malpractice—some surgeons use an 18-gauge needle for this purpose, but a 20-gauge needle is even smaller.

"Now, after he removed two to three cc's of Pantopaque, he noted a very minimal spinal fluid leak. Ordinarily, these leaks will heal spontaneously, but just to be sure, he put a small patch of Surgicel over it. Surely this couldn't be considered malpractice.

"What happened is that the spinal fluid continued to leak and eventually formed a cyst. But the true test is not one of hindsight—that is, what actually did happen—but rather, was he reasonable in expecting that the leak would self-seal? The answer to this has to be yes. Every doctor I have talked to has agreed that it was reasonable to expect the leak to heal under these circumstances. Therefore, there was no negligence and no malpractice."

Betty had been listening quietly, trying to understand. But at this point she interrupted. "How can we be sure it was only a needle puncture? Suppose he cut me accidentally? Suppose it wasn't a minimal leak, but a large leak that he should have sewn?"

Halprin was getting a little impatient. "Of course I've considered that," he said. "But he didn't cut you accidentally, and it wasn't a large leak. Clearly, if it had been, he would have done something about it. He would have sewn it up."

"Now look—" Betty was impatient too. "You know all the things that've happened to me. Would this all have happened if they did nothing wrong? You seem to think I have nothing better to do than dream all this up—"

Haskell didn't want the situation to get out of hand. "Lou," he said quietly, "isn't it just possible that the mistake we're making is that we're starting with the assumption that the doctors did nothing wrong and then looking for the evidence to back up that assumption? Maybe what we should do instead is begin with the assumption—based on Betty's condition—that they did something wrong. Suppose Betty *is* right. Suppose it *was* actually more than a small leak. After all, Dr. McReynolds is the one who describes it as 'very minimal,' and it could be that he's trying to justify his failure to sew it."

Halprin was by now thoroughly upset. He had come to the hospital expecting that he and Haskell would be on the same side. Now it began to appear that he was alone. "Look," he said, trying not to lose his temper, "even if you were right—and I know you aren't—there still would be no way in the world to prove it. Are you going to go into court and call McReynolds a liar? Are you going to say that even though he calls it a minimal leak, we know it was a big one? What evidence are you going to have to support that idea? Nobody who was in the operating room is going to testify for you. No expert is going to testify for you. There's no way you can get this case to a jury! It would be a non-suit!"

Betty wanted to know what a non-suit was. Haskell explained that it was the plaintiff's obligation to present enough proper evidence to support his contentions, and then it was up to the defendant to present his defense. However, if the judge decided that the plaintiff had failed in his obligation, it was not necessary for the defendant to present any evidence. The judge would declare the plaintiff "non-suited" and would excuse the jury. Thus, in this case, if they could not get a competent doctor to testify that in his opinion the defendant doctors had been negligent, they would not be able to present a proper case and would be non-suited.

"That's exactly what I'm saying," Halprin insisted. "I've tried, but no competent doctor will testify for us. Besides, even if we could prove negligence, it wouldn't be enough. We'd also have to prove that the negligence was the proximate cause of the injury, and in your case, Betty, it wasn't."

Halprin took two books out of his briefcase, flipped through the pages until he found what he wanted, and read aloud. According to the text, allergy to Pantopaque dye was one of the possible causes of arachnoiditis. "Now, Betty," he said, closing the books, "unfortunately, that's what happened. You had an allergic reaction. It's quite rare, but it does happen sometimes. Your original myelogram was done by Dr. Evans and Dr. Peterson, and we haven't said a word about suing them—not that it would make any difference, because there's no indication that they did anything wrong either. I'm convinced that your arachnoiditis and paralysis are due to an allergic reaction to the dye. Even if Dr. McReynolds had been negligent—and if we could prove it—we would still lose because his negligence wasn't the proximate cause of the injury.

"The defense knows as well as we do that we could never win this case, but still they're willing to pay us $10,000. Why? Well, first, I have an excellent relationship with the firm. If I were another attorney, they'd probably offer us nothing at all. And second, they would have to pay attorney fees of at least that much if we insisted on taking the case to trial. So rather than give the money to the attorneys, they're willing to give it to us. The way I see it, it's a gift, and we have no choice but to accept it. Look, I'm willing to reduce my fee from $4500 to $2500, which I'll split with Haskell. And of course the $500 that I've laid out in expenses. You'll have the rest."

Lou Halprin looked expectantly at Betty. He had given much careful consideration to this case, and had arrived at an unalterable conclusion. Why did she still hesitate? As a lay person, she could not appreciate the intricacies of the problems involved. And after all, she was paying him for his expertise and should not question the correctness of his decision.

The silence was becoming uncomfortable. At last Betty said, "I'd like to think it over."

"Damn it, Betty!" Halprin exploded. "I've been an attorney for the past ten years, and I was a doctor for twenty-one years before that. I was a specialist in internal medicine and dealt with the very same anatomy that's involved here. I've brought all my training and experience to bear in reaching this conclusion. If, in spite of all that, you still want to think it over when I tell you you have no choice, you're putting your judgment above mine, and you don't need me."

For nearly two years, in her depression, all Betty had had to look forward to was the coming battle, the trial, when she would finally see justice done. Now suddenly she saw everything being taken away from her. What did $10,000 mean? After her medical bills and attorney fees were paid, there would be nothing. Nothing but continued life in a wheelchair, a life full of pain and without either security or hope.

She looked straight at Lou Halprin and said, "You're goddam right I don't need you."

Halprin's mouth tightened. He turned to Haskell. "Well, I guess there's nothing more for us to do. Shall we go?"

Haskell hesitated. "I'd like to talk to Betty for a moment. Would you wait for me outside?"

Lou picked up his briefcase and left. When he was gone, Betty buried her face in her hands for a few seconds, then took a deep breath and said, "I guess I sure queered that one!"

"I think you made the right decision."

She looked at him in relief. "Am I glad to hear you say that! For a while there, I felt like I'd lost my last friend. Knowing you're still with me makes me feel a little better."

Haskell rose and began pacing the room. "The immediate problem is to get ready for the trial. It's only a couple of months away. I'll have to find another medical malpractice expert—it

41

won't be easy, because whoever I try to get will know that the case has already been turned down by Lou."

"Oh, you know, Haskell, I'm sick and tired of these experts. It was a couple of medical experts that got me in this fix in the first place, and it's the malpractice expert who tells me there's nothing I can do about it." She paused. "What I'd really like is for you to try the case yourself . . . if you're willing."

"But I've never tried a malpractice case in my life! Anytime I've had one, I've always turned it over to Lou."

"There's got to be a first time. You told me you tried a rape case not long ago, and you had never done that before, but you won—right? And you won a murder case, even though you'd never had one before. So what do you say?" She smiled, and her face looked more hopeful than it had in months.

Haskell Shapiro had never been one to refuse a challenge. But he wanted to be sure Betty knew what she was doing. "Remember, I lost your accident case," he said.

"As far as I'm concerned, you didn't lose that one. The jury was convinced that what was wrong with me wasn't the result of the accident, and now I'm convinced they were right."

"If that's what you want," Haskell said, "I'd be happy to represent you."

"That's what I want."

17.

June 14, 1973
Dear Lou:

Betty Burke has asked me to write to you to tell you that she does not want you to continue to represent her. She appreciates all that you have done, but obviously there is a serious personality clash between you, one that does not lend itself readily to correction.

42

She does not agree with you and she will not take your advice that her case should be settled for $10,000, although she is grateful to you for your obviously generous proposal to accept only $1,250 as attorney fees besides your costs.

Naturally, I will continue to represent her. I would appreciate it if you would prepare and execute a Substitution of Attorneys.

Haskell

June 18, 1973
Dear Haskell:

Betty Burke, of course, is entirely free to do whatever she elects. The problem in her case remains as it did before, being able to have the case submitted to the jury. To date, although I have devoted many hours to that problem including a trip to Santa Barbara and one to Downey, I have not succeeded in obtaining any testimony that would accomplish that purpose.

As a matter of interest, I reviewed the facts in the case with another physician friend of mine this weekend. Although we agreed that her condition resulted from the sequence of events that occurred in 1967 and that the myelogram and the surgery were the contributing factors, we were not able to agree as to whether there was any evidence of negligence. The holdup still remains that arachnoiditis may follow a myelogram and that is a risk that must be assumed by the patient. As you know, we did not sue the doctor who performed the myelogram because the statute had run out.

Lou

June 29, 1973
Dear Haskell:

Enclosed please find the Substitution of Attorneys that Mrs. Burke has requested.

With respect to my last letter to you, please understand that the entire problem in this case is that of obtaining a doctor to testify. With a doctor the trial is easy—without one it is impossible.

Incidentally, I have talked to several more doctors about the matter and have not yet had anyone state that there was negligence and/or proximate cause.

Lou

18.

In early July, 1973, Haskell received a phone call from a young lawyer named David Sabih whom he had met socially a few years before. Sabih said he had just passed the bar exam, and needed some advice as to what direction his career should take.

One thing was certain: whatever direction his career took, he would be successful. David Sabih had been born in Iraq, and had lived there and in Israel until he was eighteen. His background was different from Haskell's—he was the only child of a wealthy family who gave him whatever he wanted. But he was similar to Haskell in an important respect: he never doubted that he would succeed at whatever he put his hand to. When he applied for entrance to the university, even though only five of each thousand applicants were accepted, he knew he would be one of them. And like Haskell, he was the youngest student at the university.

He studied engineering, and came to the U. S. as an exchange student, studying at C.C.N.Y., M.I.T. and U.C.L.A., from which he received his Ph.D. in 1958. He worked as an engineer for Hughes Aircraft until 1964, and then, feeling it was time for a change—by now he was married and had a family, and wanted to make more money—went into real estate. Since there were a thousand people moving to California every day, he reasoned, that was obviously the field for him.

By 1969, David Sabih was a millionaire. Then he decided

it was time for another change, so he started law school. While still a law student, he sued the California Pacific Leasing Company for camouflaging a usurious rate of interest. He served as his own lawyer, won the case, and was awarded $650,000. The verdict made the front page of the *New York Times*. But the judge, deciding that the jury had been "led by passion and prejudice," overturned the decision, and the case was finally settled for $50,000.

David Sabih and Haskell met for lunch. Though he had been in the United States for eighteen years and considered himself an American, David still had an accent and a decidedly foreign way of speaking. He was a short and rather chunky man with a wild crop of curly black hair, a black mustache, and an apologetic manner that did not quite hide his absolute self-confidence and razor-sharp mind. Over luncheon at Benihana's in Los Angeles, they discussed his prospects.

Haskell sensed immediately that this young man's intelligence and tireless energy would be an enormous asset in the Betty Burke case. He told David the story. Would he be interested in working on it? Should they win, there might be a very substantial award; however, realistically speaking, the odds were against them.

David was very much interested. The question of the odds did not trouble him; he liked challenges.

They agreed that Haskell would pay him $100 per day for his work; and if they should win the case, an additional, retroactive $200 per day.

David Sabih immediately set to work with the diligence and thoroughness that had gotten him an engineering doctorate at the age of 21, and a real estate fortune at 32.

19.

"Anyone familiar with cases of this character knows that the so-called ethical practitioner will not testify on behalf of a plaintiff regardless of the merits of his case. This is largely due to the pressure exerted by medical societies and public liability insurance companies which issue policies of liability insurance to physicians covering malpractice claims. . . . Regardless of the merits of the plaintiff's case, physicians who are members of medical societies flock to the defense of their fellow member charged with malpractice, and the plaintiff is relegated, for his expert testimony, to the occasional lone wolf or heroic soul, who for the sake of truth and justice has the courage to run the risk of ostracism by his fellow practitioners and the cancellation of his public liability insurance policy."

Are these the complaining words of a frustrated and bitter plaintiff's lawyer? On the contrary. They were spoken by a respected judge, the Honorable Jesse Carter of the Supreme Court of California, in the case of *Huffman v. Lindquist,* 1951.

It has long been recognized that a "conspiracy of silence" exists among many doctors who refuse to testify against other doctors in malpractice suits. A survey was done a few years ago of 214 doctors at the Boston University Law Medical Research Institute. They were asked, "Would you be willing to appear in court for the patient where a surgeon, operating for a diseased kidney, removed the wrong one?" Only 27% of the general practitioners and 31% of the specialists said yes.

One of twenty-one "commandments" in the Journal of the American Medical Association is "The physician must avoid destructive and unethical criticism of the work of other physicians." On the other hand, the AMA's *Principles of Medical Ethics* says, "A physician should expose, without fear or favor, incompetent or corrupt, dishonest or unethical conduct on the part of members of the profession." Far too often, doctors take the first statement as their creed and conveniently forget the second. They give many reasons for their reluctance to testify against one another: defendants may be found negligent when in fact no negligence has occurred; the inexact nature of the science of medicine makes the definition of a reasonable standard of care vague and elusive; jurors, who are laymen, may not be competent to decide complex medical questions; doctors may be censured or ostracized by medical societies; their insurance premiums may be increased or cancelled (there have been cases in which malpractice rates have jumped as much as 200% after a plaintiff won as little as $20,000); feelings of professional loyalty must not be violated for any but the grossest violations of good practice.

Despite the fears of doctors, malpractice is very hard to prove. The physician has the advantages of knowledge and position, and for the most part, the confidence and trust of the public. The plaintiff has the burden of establishing the standard of care required of the physician, as well as the physician's violation of that standard. The obvious way, and the way required by law, for the plaintiff to do this, is to obtain expert medical testimony. When, as often happens, he is unable to obtain a qualified physician willing to testify, he may be nonsuited for failing to establish a proper case. If he does manage to obtain testimony, it may be that of physicians less qualified than those who are available to the defendant.

A doctor is not required by law to guarantee the success of his work. The law recognizes that doctors are human, and that human beings make mistakes. Doctors are required only to use reasonable judgment and skill in accordance with the standard prevailing in their community. The defendant doctor can expect the jury's sympathies to be with him. Heard frequently among jurors are statements like "No matter what we do, the plaintiff's condition will remain the same, but our verdict can ruin the doctor"; "If you can't trust your doctor, why did you go to him in the first place?"; "Doctors go to school for a long time, who are we to pass judgment on them?"; "If doctors are going to be sued, they will never dare treat anyone." Cocktail-party conversations deplore the enormous verdicts awarded in malpractice cases, which make it prohibitive for doctors to pay their insurance premiums. What most people haven't heard about is the vast number of cases that never get to a jury at all, because the plaintiff cannot find a doctor courageous enough to brave the wrath of his professional brethren, as well as of the insurance companies, and testify to what he believes is the truth.

Recently, there have been a few legal developments that have made it a little easier for a plaintiff to crack the "conspiracy of silence." One is the doctrine of *res ipsa loquitur*, "the thing speaks for itself." This applies in cases where such obvious professional incompetence exists that a layman would have no difficulty in recognizing it—instances of instruments left in the abdomen after surgery, x-ray burns received during diagnosis, infection that can clearly be traced to the use of non-sterile instruments, a healthy part of the body injured during an operation for an unrelated condition, or the wrong organ removed. In cases such as these, the plaintiff does not need a doctor's testimony to establish a case. But *res ipsa loquitur* is useless in the more subtle—and commoner—types of malpractice, such as failure to follow a patient's condition post-surgically; improper reading of x-rays; lack of informed consent (the need for patients to be adequately informed of the risks of treatment); failure to write proper orders for medication and treatment; performance of surgery that may be unnecessary; injections improperly given; prescription of drugs without full awareness of their side effects or contraindications.

Other developments in the direction of breaking the conspiracy are the use of medical texts to establish a *prima facie* case when expert testimony is not available; the use of the defendant's doctor's testimony to establish the expert testimony the plaintiff needs; and the enlargement of the concept of the "community" with whose standard of care the expert doctor must be familiar—thus making potential witnesses of many doctors who, if the community were limited to a town or part of a town, would be disqualified.

48

But despite these developments, defeating the conspiracy in each individual case requires a herculean effort on the part of the attorney for the plaintiff. Lou Halprin had been unwilling or unable to make that effort. In two years he had not found one doctor who would testify that there had been negligence in the case of Betty Burke.

David Sabih in two weeks found two such doctors.

20.

The first physician who indicated his willingness to testify for the plaintiff was Dr. William Cooper, a neurologist. He believed that the continued leak of spinal fluid after Betty's first operation had allowed bacteria from the bedsheets to enter the wound, probably causing a low-grade infection that ultimately resulted in arachnoiditis.

David consulted a lawyer in Sacramento who had tried a number of arachnoiditis cases. The lawyer thought Betty had a good case. He offered to provide a neurosurgeon who would testify that arachnoiditis occurs *only* if there is negligence. The neurosurgeon's fee would be $10,000. There was a catch, however: he would be made available only if the lawyer were brought in on the case on a 50–50 basis. David declined the offer.

On July 25, David went to interview Dr. Mooney, who had assisted Dr. McReynolds in the first and second operations. The first thing he noticed was that Drs. McReynolds and Mooney shared a suite of offices, and that Dr. Spindle's office was in the same building. He reported:

From the layout of these offices and from my impression, it is obvious that Spindle, McReynolds and Mooney are involved in a joint professional enterprise.

49

It would be foolish to expect that Dr. Mooney would testify against his friend, colleague and partner, Dr. McReynolds. Indeed, Dr. Mooney was suspicious of me and my motives and agreed to the interview very reluctantly and conducted himself apprehensively. He spoke very highly of Dr. McReynolds' professional ability. Dr. Mooney pretended that he did not recall the various details of Betty Burke's case, although he was familiar with the name. He did not recall if he assisted McReynolds in one or more operations on Betty. He says he is suspicious of all lawyers and indicated his disappointment and distress for the involvement of Dr. McReynolds in this litigation. After awhile I was able to put Dr. Mooney at ease, even though he compared me to Colombo, and I was able to elicit the following information:

During all of his medical practice he never had to participate in a second operation (as was the case with Betty Burke) and he considers the need for the second operation probably very unusual and rare, one in a thousand. I believe such a statement, if elicited on the witness stand, can be used in an argument to the jury as follows: "If Dr. McReynolds had operated on Betty Burke without any negligence and in a high professional standard, it is obvious there would have been no need for a second operation. Indeed, his own associate claims that there is only one in a thousand chances for a need for a second operation. Well, I will tell you, ladies and gentlemen, that this means that there was only one in a thousand chances that Dr. McReynolds was not negligent."

David asked Dr. Mooney what size hole a 20-gauge needle would create. About a half a millimeter, he said. David told him the hole created by Dr. McReynolds' needle had been ⅛ of an inch. "He expressed amazement," David reported, "but it was obvious that he was trying to protect his friend McReynolds when he started hedging that the stress of the needle may have created a larger hole."

Dr. Peter Rabin, one of the doctors Lou Halprin had consulted, had refused to testify for the plaintiff, but had agreed to write a report on Betty Burke. When David went to see him on July 30 to obtain that report, however, Dr. Rabin had changed his mind. David reported to Haskell:

> Dr. Rabin stated that he would not write to you any report concerning Betty Burke since he is a friend of numerous other doctors who are friends of Dr. McReynolds. He discussed the dilemma with his wife, and they both made the decision not to cooperate in this case.

Dr. Rabin told David that his wife played bridge with Dr. McReynolds' wife. Nevertheless, David managed, in his apologetic "Colombo" manner, to extract some significant remarks from Dr. Rabin:

> He stated that the ⅛-inch hole must have been, in fact, ¼ inch, as indicated by the number of sutures which were necessary to sew it. He felt that Dr. McReynolds tore the dura and did not close the opening properly. He said the problems of Betty Burke stem from the fact that blood leaked into the opening and caused the arachnoiditis. He said your theory that infection set in cannot be sustained, since there was no clinical proof that any infection was noticed during the second, third or fourth operations.

Dr. Rabin admitted that he doubted the defendant's contention that Betty's condition resulted from the myelogram. Only if there had been a bloody tap when the myelogram was performed could any problem have arisen, he said. David recalled that Dr. McReynolds' deposition made no mention of blood in connection with the myelogram.

51

David and Haskell found their second expert witness in Dr. Michael Sukoff, who was interviewed on July 27th. After reading the depositions of Betty Burke, Flora Hoover and Dr. McReynolds, he said that, in his opinion, Dr. McReynolds was negligent in removing the Pantopaque during the operation, since this is widely recognized as a source of possible complications. He noted that Dr. McReynolds changed Betty's position during the removal of the dye; this might have enlarged the hole. The dural tear, he felt, should have been sutured; and the Surgicel served no useful purpose whatever. The necessity of a second operation, he said, was evidence of negligence in the performance of the first operation. And the third and fourth operations should never have been done at all, since, given the patient's history, they could only do more harm than good.

21.

I felt very confident in the way the case was being handled. David— the things that man did on my case! He got into it tooth and nail. He actually got permission to watch an operation! That man knew as much, when he got in that courtroom, as any neurosurgeon. He has a fantastic mind. And he cares. And of course Haskell, through all of it, stood by me.

David began his research by ordering reprints of articles in medical journals and immersing himself in medical textbooks. He learned that arachnoiditis is one of the most mysterious of diseases. It occurs sometimes as a result of spinal cord disease, sometimes as a result of hemorrhage, infection or trauma. It can follow the injection of Pantopaque dye, spinal anesthetics or other substances, or the removal of tumors. It is usually difficult, if not impossible, to pinpoint the exact cause of arachnoiditis, and equally difficult or impossible to do anything about it once the scar tissue has formed. Re-operation is seldom successful, since scar tissue always re-forms. Some doctors treat arachnoiditis with intraspinal injections of Novocain and corticosteroids, followed by exercises designed to stretch the adhesions around the nerve roots.

He learned that the spinal cord is something like a telephone cable, with hundreds of thousands of wires that conduct impulses from the legs or arms up and from the brain down. The cord is surrounded by cerebro-spinal fluid, which is held in bounds by the dura, which is in turn protected by bone. The dural sac is actually made up of three layers: the dura mater (hard mother), a tough, fibrous membrane; the arachnoid, lying within the dura, a semi-transparent filamentous layer (its name indicates that it is like a spider's web); and the pia mater (tender mother), the innermost and the softest of the three layers. When the arachnoid is disturbed or traumatized, the cells that produce fibrous tissue to promote healing undergo a reactive process, and there is scar formation. The arachnoid becomes "stuck" to the nerves; the adhesions engulf and incorporate the nerves and squeeze them. The nerve roots then become irritated and may be partially or completely destroyed, as manifested by muscle atrophy, loss of sensation, loss of bowel or bladder control.

David Sabih read also that dural cysts, while rare, occur occasionally in patients who have undergone laminectomies and in whom the dural closure was not watertight. In one article he found the significant statement that "the formation of a dural cyst should be prevented by meticulous closure of the dural defect." And in another: "There is a good indication that persistence of a small dural defect is most apt to lead to cyst formation. Therefore, known defects should be closed in a secure fashion." This would be excellent ammunition at the trial.

One item he came across in his research started a new train of thought in his mind: it is common practice in the United States to remove virtually all of the Pantopaque dye directly after a myelogram, leaving only a few droplets that could never be removed entirely. But Dr. McReynolds had insisted all along that during the first operation he had removed 2 or 3 cc. of Pantopaque from Betty's spine. Why would the radiologist who performed the myelogram have gone contrary to the accepted procedure and left the dye in?

The matter of the Surgicel bothered David. Dr. Mooney had shown some uncertainty about the effectiveness of Surgicel in stopping a spinal fluid leak.

He discussed it with Haskell, who asked a friend of his, Dr. Hyman Cantor, to get a package of Surgicel for him. Haskell studied the brochure very carefully. Surgicel was described as "an oxidized regenerated cellulose developed specifically for the control of capillary or venous bleeding or small arterial hemorrhage where conventional means of control are technically impractical." Further along: "When Surgicel comes into contact with whole blood at the site of a wound, an artificially induced clot forms rapidly in the vicinity of the product and local hemorrhage is readily controlled." The brochure went on to spell out in great detail the uses of Surgicel in general, cardiovascular, neurological and dental surgery, as well as contraindications, warnings, precautions and adverse reactions. It stressed that Surgicel was "not meant as a substitute for careful surgery and the proper use of sutures and ligatures." Haskell was jubilant when he read: "It should be emphasized that Surgicel must be in contact with whole blood to be effective. Other body fluids, such as serum, have not been found to react with Surgicel to produce a satisfactory hemostatic effect." Spinal fluid, he had learned, was mostly water—98%, in fact. Surely then, he reasoned, when spinal fluid came into contact with whole blood, the blood would become diluted and could no longer be considered "whole blood." It seemed logical that the Surgicel could not be effective. This ought to be clear evidence of negligence.

In looking over the brochure again, he happened to notice that the date on it was 1970. Betty's first two operations had been in 1967.

22.

September 5, 1973
Dear Haskell:

Some time ago, my very dear friend for the past 25 years, Lou Halprin, came in to talk with me about a most distressing situation. It involves a client of yours, a Mrs. Betty Burke.

I know you are familiar with the facts. There is an overriding issue that is concerning Lou and about which he spoke with me. It is his feeling that the present tragic condition from which Mrs. Burke is suffering is most probably related to the administration of Pantopaque in a myelographic study performed in the early part of 1967.

A review of the facts would indicate that the statute of limitations has run as to the doctor who performed the myelography.

The very troublesome question that remains is whether or not, in filing a malpractice suit against Dr. McReynolds, who performed a laminectomy, there should have been a joinder of the doctor who did the myelogram. From my point of view, there appears to be no question but that that doctor should have been sued within the required four-year period. From a trial point of view, I cannot, of course, state that such a filing would insure a recovery. But I can state that the failure to sue all necessary defendants constitutes a genuine flaw in the presentation of the present case, particularly when the suit is predicated on professional negligence.

Dr. McReynolds and his group are extremely sophisticated orthopedists, who have an intimate knowledge of arachnoiditis and other entities of that nature.

In the light of the foregoing, Lou was very concerned

about whether he had a duty to disclose to his former client the necessity for having joined the doctor who performed the study referred to. On this issue, I felt the conclusion was inescapable. Lou was duty-bound to make a full disclosure to the client, and, of course, this leads to your personal involvement.

You can gather that this is not an easy letter to write. Silence is often a most commendable quality. Out of my respect for you, I hesitate to get involved. But under the circumstances, I felt constrained to advise Lou that it was his duty as a lawyer to make a full disclosure to his former client.

I'll be happy to discuss this matter with you at any time that is convenient but, as you can gather, time is of the essence, and if you feel you wish to discuss it with me, please don't hesitate to call.

Sincerely yours,
Raoul

Raoul Magaña was a well-known personal-injury lawyer, a close friend and associate of Lou Halprin's. With Halprin, he had collaborated on a number of important books and articles in the field of legal medicine. It was mainly on Magaña's account that Halprin had decided to study law after being a physician for twenty-one years.

It seemed fairly clear to Haskell that Halprin had never dreamed Betty would ignore his advice, or that Haskell would press on with the case. And although Halprin had been supremely confident that the case would never come before a jury, it seemed he was now beginning to think otherwise. Juries were notoriously unpredictable. . . . Suppose Betty were to win the case? That would be a terrible embarrassment to Lou Halprin, the eminent malpractice specialist, who had decided the case didn't have a chance. However, if something had been done wrong in preparing the case—if, say, there had been a failure to sue all possible defendants, and if the attorney, in failing to tell his client about this mistake, had been guilty of ethical misconduct—then the case might be prevented from ever coming to court. So Lou Halprin had gone to his good friend Raoul Magaña and "confessed" his deep concern over the flaw in the case.

Haskell made an appointment with Magaña and went to his office. He had decided to say nothing about what Lou's motivations might be; he wanted only to set Magaña's mind at rest about any question of misconduct. They exchanged pleasantries and plunged into the rather awkward matter at hand.

"In this case, Raoul, it would have been a mistake to include Evans and Peterson, the doctors who did the myelogram. According to our theory of the case, the myelogram did *not* cause the arachnoiditis. It had nothing to do with it."

"That isn't what Lou thinks. And I can't help agreeing with him. In cases of diffused arachnoiditis such as this—"

"But Betty's arachnoiditis isn't diffused; it's localized in one area."

Raoul was surprised. "Lou gave me the impression that it *was* diffused. If he knows it's localized, he must surely realize that the Pantopaque could not have caused it. But in any case, you ought to have informed your client of the reasons for not suing Drs. Evans and Peterson."

Haskell smiled. "I've already discussed it with her, and she agrees. And as for the matter of time being of the essence—well, time was certainly of the essence while Lou was handling the case, but it took him nearly two years to decide there was no case."

"All right, I wish you luck. From what I've heard about this case, I think you'll need it. This *is* your first malpractice case, isn't it?"

"That's right. And it's the very first case my assistant, David Sabih, has handled since he passed the bar. I only hope our ignorance doesn't show too much."

September 19, 1973
Dear Haskell:
First, I want to express my appreciation to you for the

57

very courteous treatment you extended to me in a matter that was as delicate as this.

I had the privilege of speaking with Mrs. Burke. She sounded like a very lovely and wonderful person. She likes you very much and agrees that you have worked very, very hard on her matter. I, of course, told her that every desire you and I and Lou had was to see her win her case.

In my discussion with Lou, I told him that there was no need for any further worry on his part, that you had taken up the matter cleanly and clearly with Mrs. Burke, that you had explained the fact that the doctor who took the original myelogram was not in the lawsuit and that there was always the possibility that the defendants would blame all of the arachnoiditis on the original myelogram.

I am sure you will find that Lou will be extremely cooperative with you, should the occasion arise, and that he will do nothing that will impair Mrs. Burke's rights.

With all good wishes,
Raoul

PART TWO

PART TWO

1.

"The importance of the settlement conference judge in bringing about a settlement of a case cannot be overemphasized. Time and time again, I have had the experience of a Mandatory Conference beginning in chambers with the plaintiff's lawyer and the defendant's lawyer each stating that a settlement was impossible in the case because they were too far apart on both the issues of liability and damages. To some judges, such an announcement has no effect. These judges take the attitude that the impossible case is just as subject to reaching a satisfactory settlement as any other case. It has been my experience that many such impossible cases have been settled because the conference judge has been willing to take the time and make the effort to bring about a settlement. In such a situation, the easy way out is for the conference judge to accept the statement of counsel that the case is impossible of settlement and send the parties away to go to trial on the established trial date. An effective settlement conference judge refuses to take this easy approach.

".... A factor of importance in producing a settlement is adequate preparation for the Mandatory Settlement Conference on the part of all counsel. . . .

"Another essential ingredient for the success of a Mandatory Settlement Conference is that all parties shall be present whose consent is required for a settlement. . . . If a defendant is insured, it is the presence of a claims representative of the insurance carrier that is important."

—Judge Bernard S. Jefferson
Los Angeles Superior Court
quoted in Los Angeles Trial Lawyers
Assoc. *Advocate,* July, 1973

61

The attorneys for the plaintiff and the defendants in the case of *Burke vs. McReynolds, et al.* met for the Mandatory Settlement Conference in the chambers of the settlement judge some three weeks before the start of the trial. Haskell Shapiro had already spoken on the phone with Wallace Reed, who was defending Drs. McReynolds and Spindle, and had expressed his opinion that since the two sides were so far apart, there was probably little chance for a settlement. Wallace Reed did not agree. His firm was prepared to negotiate, he said. He considered that there was an excellent chance to reach an agreement, if not at the first settlement conference, then at a second—or a third.

Haskell Shapiro went to the conference prepared for protracted and difficult negotiations. He was armed with a lengthy brief that David had prepared: it included the history of the four operations; an estimate of damages to the plaintiff in loss of earnings, pain and suffering, and medical costs past and future; a discussion of the acts of negligence which the plaintiff hoped to prove and of the merits of her case; hospital records and various other relevant documents.

Wallace Reed did not attend the conference. In his place, the firm of Kirtland and Packard had sent another lawyer—one, Haskell Shapiro knew, who was lower on the firm's totem pole. He came with no brief, no documents. The representative of the doctors' insurance company, the man who actually held the purse strings, did not attend.

Despite what Wallace Reed had said, his stand-in stated positively that his firm was not prepared to raise the original offer of $10,000, the offer that Lou Halprin had wanted Betty to accept.

"My client cannot accept $10,000," Haskell replied.

"Well then," said the judge, as though grateful to have the matter disposed of so simply, "we'll have to go to trial."

Shortly before it was due to start, Haskell heard from Harold Hunter, another attorney with the defense firm. He had taken over the case from Wallace Reed, and he said he felt it would be a mistake not to settle the case out of court. Why didn't they get together and discuss it?

Hunter and Haskell met for lunch at the Norwalk Courthouse cafeteria. Harold Hunter was a dark-haired, serious, thoughtful man, not quick to smile, slow and deliberate of speech but highly articulate. He spoke without the hesitations, the "wells" and "uhs" that punctuate the speech of most people. A specialist in professional liability cases, he had had many years of experience in the successful defense of physicians charged with malpractice.

Harold Hunter was well aware that Halprin, for whose reputation as a malpractice expert he had great respect, had turned down the case and advised his client to accept $10,000. He was confident the case could be successfully defended if it came to trial, but he hoped to save his clients distress and publicity by settling, if at all possible.

"We are willing to go as high as $60,000," he told Haskell.

The plaintiff's lawyer smiled. "Well, Harold," he began, "if you were talking about a quarter of a million, there might be something for us to discuss. Now I'm not saying we would accept it, but we would consider it."

"You can't be serious," replied Harold Hunter.

"Oh, but I am," said Haskell Shapiro, still smiling.

2.

"I came into the whole thing with the idea in my mind that too many people are suing their doctors every time the opportunity arises and getting their cases decided in their favor. So I possibly had a wee bit of prejudice. I think a lot of people are just sitting around looking for an opportunity to sue people as a way of making money. I've heard of some people that make it a practice to go into the hospital and sue. Now I feel there has to be some way of keeping control on your doctor; you can't just set them up as little tin gods and say 'I don't know anything, you go ahead'—because there is too much opportunity for them to become just that, a little tin god whose word is law. But too many people, when they find they've gambled and lost, don't want to accept their responsibilities. I definitely have faith in doctors. I feel they're the best solution we have to our ills. Without them, what would we do?"

—Bob Siemann, juror
aged 40, rodman and chainman
for a land-surveying
company

3.

SUPERIOR COURT FOR THE COUNTY OF LOS ANGELES, NORWALK, CALIFORNIA. SEPTEMBER 21, 1973.

The courtroom looks very much like any other: large, bare, dingy and forbidding, with the judge's massive bench and comfortable leather chair at the far wall, looking like an altar for the worship of justice. To the judge's left is the witness stand, to his right the jury box; in front of him are the two large attorneys' tables; beyond them the railed-off seats for spectators, witnesses, extra jurors.

The stage is set for the second act of a drama of which the dénouement is unknown; a drama in which there is no script, only a few stage directions; in which the actors do not drop their roles when they leave the theater. Betty Burke will not get up and walk away from her wheelchair once she is off the stage.

The Honorable William E. McGinley is a distinguished-looking middle-aged man, slim but well-built, with slightly receding brown hair; a cautious, conservative man who tends to go by the book and, when in doubt, to opt for the traditional way of doing things.

64

The attorneys for the plaintiff and the defendants enter the judge's chambers to acquaint him with the case.

"Is there any chance of a settlement?" the judge asks the attorneys.

"None at this time, Your Honor."

In the courtroom, the pool of forty or fifty prospective jurors waits nervously to learn their fate, wondering—some in hope, but most in dread—if they will be among those chosen to devote their lives for the next several days (weeks, perhaps?) to the matter of *Burke v. McReynolds et al.*

The judge briefly summarizes the case for the potential jurors: it is alleged by the plaintiff that her paralysis has been caused by the negligence of her physicians. He then instructs the bailiff to swear the prospective jurors for the *voir dire*, the examination that is supposed to determine their fitness to sit in judgment on the case at hand. They all raise their right hands and swear that they will answer truthfully all questions put to them. The bailiff then picks fourteen names (including two alternates) out of a basket, and the lucky, or unlucky, ones take their places in the jury box.

The judge questions them. He asks their names, their addresses, their occupations and their spouses' occupations. Are any of them in poor health or desirous of being excused for some other reason? If they are, they do not say so. Do they all speak and understand English? They do.

David Sabih questions the jury as a whole: would anyone object to giving a large sum of money for pain and suffering? Is anyone a member of a group that denies the existence of pain and suffering? Would they be swayed in their judgment by sympathy for either side? No juror will admit that he or she might be swayed. Have they any relatives who are doctors or lawyers? Have they ever had a back injury? Do they have any relatives who have disabilities similar to Betty's, or who have had back surgery?

One man raises his hand.

"Your name?"

"Bob Siemann." His father had a back operation, he says.

"What was the result of the operation?"

"He died."

"Would you then say that you might be prejudiced against doctors?"

"Oh, no. It wasn't the doctor's fault at all. I have great faith in doctors."

David Sabih and Haskell Shapiro confer on whether they should excuse this man. Both sides are permitted eight "peremptory challenges"—they may remove eight jurors without giving specific cause. They confer also with Dr. Albert Mehrabian, a psychologist from the University of California, whom they have retained to help them in the selection of jurors. Dr. Mehrabian has been carefully observing each potential juror's facial expressions, gestures, dress, inflections, "body language" —all signs, to him, of which way the individual juror is likely to go. Certain ones he has already pointed out as bad risks for the plaintiff: those who seem reserved, introverted, "uptight," and might be reluctant to award a substantial sum of money; those who appear particularly self-confident and self-reliant and who might be likely to reason that since they don't need to be paid for their problems, no one else does, either. Such people are excused by the plaintiff's attorneys. On the other hand, there are a few who appear to Dr. Mehrabian to be sympathetic, generous, outgoing— happy people who would like to see Betty Burke win a great deal of money. These, he predicts, will be dismissed by the attorney for the defendants. And, in fact, his predictions turn out to be remarkably accurate.

Dr. Mehrabian recommends that Bob Siemann be retained. Mr. Siemann may be somewhat prejudiced in favor of doctors, but the fact that he readily admits his feelings augurs well. People who radiate honesty, as he does, are likely to try almost painfully hard to be fair and impartial.

It takes a little over two days to select the jury. The jurors are all white, middle-class, evenly divided between men and women. They are salespeople, accountants, housewives, a law student; they range in age from a girl of twenty to a man in his sixties. The law student is a veteran juror, but most have never served on a jury before and are excited, apprehensive and perhaps a bit resentful at this interruption of their normal lives.

The jury is sworn: they hold up their right hands again and swear not to discuss the case with anyone, and not to make up their minds until they have heard all the evidence and received the instructions that the judge will give them.

The trial begins on September 25, 1973.

4.

In his opening statement, David Sabih outlined the main points of the plaintiff's case: that Dr. McReynolds operated on Betty too hastily and without adequately informing her of the risks involved in the surgery; that the dural defect should have been sutured and not patched with Surgicel; that the Pantopaque dye Dr. McReynolds claimed to have removed had in fact not been there; that the second operation should have been performed as soon as the leak of spinal fluid was discovered; that the third operation probably should not have been done at all, but that in any case Dr. Spindle had done it too quickly and had severed functional nerves; that a Silastic tube should not have been used in the fourth operation; that this last surgery also was probably unnecessary and was done too quickly and without adequate optical magnification.

David Sabih spoke for about half an hour. Harold Hunter's opening statement was much briefer: he would show that there was no negligence at all and that whatever was done by the two surgeons was within the standard of care accepted by the community; that nothing either doctor did was the proximate cause of Betty Burke's disability; and that Dr. Spindle, particularly, was exempt from liability because any damage Betty had sustained, from whatever cause, had already occurred before he came into the case.

The first witnesses for the plaintiff were Charles and Doris Spears. They had known Betty Burke for many years, and talked about her activities as a girl and young woman.

When I was about seventeen or eighteen, my girlfriend Cindy and I decided to learn to fly. We took lessons at the Salinas Airport. You have to do about six hours with the instructor before you can fly solo. Then an older fellow who kept his private plane there let me use it for solo flying.

Cindy and I were the only two female students in the whole Bay area, Monterey and San Francisco. It even got into the newspapers. And that was long before Women's Lib.

One time I was flying with the instructor when there was some problem with the carburetion or something. We had to make a forced landing in a beet field near Gonzalez. I said, that's it, I'll never fly again. And as it turned out, I didn't. But not because I didn't want to. I just got into other things—marriage and things—and got away from it. But I loved it, it was fantastic. I guess my flying days are over, though.

I used to take part in rodeos. They had them all year long, just all the time, it was more or less a way of life. I'd be in the barrel races where you race your horse around a barrel for speed, in competition. And I'd go to the ropings—there I was just a spectator, of course. Or I'd be a pick-up girl. That's where you ride in to pick up the guys who fall off the bucking broncos; you get 'em up on your horse behind you, so they don't get trampled.

Edna Taylor, Betty's mother, took the stand. Mrs. Taylor was a crusty, tough-talking old lady, with a deeply lined face and an air of determination. She had had to quit her job as a bookkeeper in order to take care of Betty, she said, because Betty's husband had left her.

She testified that Dr. McReynolds had not seen Betty until the night before the first operation. He had said it was a very simple operation. Nothing to worry about.

Yes, she had seen that Betty's sheets were wet with spinal fluid. No, Dr. McReynolds had not been around between the first and second operations.

Dr. Spindle had not seen Betty until the night before surgery either. He had been very reassuring, too, had told

Betty and Mrs. Taylor not to worry.

Yes, Betty was in pain almost every day. She could not sit up for more than an hour without excruciating pain.

Harold Hunter cross-examined. Did a bookcase fall on Betty prior to her first operation? It did. Did she undergo a myelogram prior to the first operation? She did. Had there been trouble in Betty's marriage before her back problems? Yes. In fact, was Gene Burke an alcoholic? Yes. Had Mrs. Taylor testified at the auto accident trial that her daughter had been fine until the accident? She didn't remember.

The next witness was Betty's brother Everett, a lean, rangy man with a pronounced Western drawl. He strode to the stand with the bow-legged walk of a cowboy and looked as though he would be far more at ease on a horse than in a courtroom. He said Gene Burke's drinking had increased as a result of Betty's condition. It was true that they had separated once before Betty's first surgery; but this was certainly not unusual. He felt that they'd had no greater problems than any couple might have when one partner has a drinking problem.

Yes, he and his sister were very close.

Everett took me to Disneyland after I was in the wheelchair. We took my mother and the kids, and we really got the royal treatment, even before we got in—you get special parking. And we didn't wait in any lines. As soon as they see there's someone in a wheelchair, somebody comes out and gets you and your whole party and you go right into the ride or the exhibit or whatever. We saw the "Small World," and the Lincoln Exhibit, and the Steamboat, and the "Pirates of the Caribbean." And we had a lovely dinner at the hotel.

All my first outings after I was in the chair—Everett always took me. I just felt safe with him. The public rest rooms were always quite an ordeal. But Everett would just open the door of the ladies' room and yell "Clear out!" and then he'd carry me in.

He took me bowling several times. I'd just roll the chair up to the line, my son would bring me the ball, and I'd let 'er rip. I had quite a high average. It's quite common for people in wheelchairs to bowl.

After I got out of Rehab I had to stay with Everett for a while. I couldn't get in the bathroom at all without being carried in. And the only way I could take a bath was if he put me in the tub.

Betty Burke's two stepsons, Mitchell and Larry, testified that their father's drinking had increased since Betty had become paralyzed. Mitchell, who was fourteen, said he had left home because of the drinking, but that he was attached to Betty and wanted to live with her.

Larry, eighteen, said he had left school and was fixing Betty's house in order to sell it.

Was Betty like a natural mother to him? "Yes." Did his father ever use Betty's condition to hurt her? "He called her a cripple."

Gene had made three or four attempts on his life and was in and out of the Sanitarium several times. He was out at the time of the auto accident trial, but there was really no time when he wasn't either drunk or working on getting drunk or sleeping off a drunk. We just learned to live around it, the kids and I—to function without him.

We still lived together till just before the malpractice trial. But then he started playing around with other women, publicly and disgustingly, till it reached the point where the children were even ashamed to go down to the beach and talk to their friends.

I didn't have any problem with sex until after the 1969 surgery. It created all kinds of problems with my husband, because even though I still had the equipment, he didn't feel—because I didn't get any satisfaction, it was not the same to him, either. We tried other types of sex . . . it was a problem. Although, actually, he'd gotten to where he was drunk so much of the time sex didn't matter much to him.

Now I'm really starting to confront the sex issue. I have a desire for sex, but no ability for it. If I meet a guy that turns me on, I have to realize that there's nothing I can do about it.

While I was in the Rehab Center, Gene wanted to sell the house and get an apartment so he could bring me home and take care of me. And he had been real good to me, cooking meals and even cleaning up after me. But I had decided some time previously that as far as our marriage was concerned, it was over. It was really over long before the break-up. When you lose respect for somebody, love goes too. All my emotion for him was spent long ago.

70

So I said, don't do me any favors. Don't plan on an apartment for both of us. I'm sure you really want out, and I know that's what I want.

Well, the idea of being a swinging bachelor again grabbed him, which was understandable.

5.

"We became aware of how sensitive an operation back surgery is. And even a myelogram, that I don't think a lot of people would give too much thought to—now I don't want one, myself. But what penetrated most was the seriousness of back surgery and how careful you should be in how you select a doctor and what you should find out first, things you should ask. We've probably all had trouble with doctors over that, because you go to a doctor and start asking questions, and they become unhappy with you."

—Emma Oaks, juror
aged 50, salesclerk

About a week after the beginning of the trial, one of the jurors began complaining of back pain, and was excused.

Dr. Chester Cornell McReynolds was a tall, thin man of about sixty-five, slightly stooped, with glasses, salt-and-pepper gray hair and a bushy gray mustache. Well-groomed and soft-spoken, he radiated kindliness and sincerity. His face was deeply lined. He seldom smiled.

"You do solemnly swear that the testimony you may give in the cause now pending before this court shall be the truth, the whole truth, and nothing but the truth, so help you God?"

"I do."

"Will you be seated, sir. State your full name."

"Chester Cornell McReynolds."

"Dr. McReynolds, what is your business or occupation?"

"I am a medical doctor."

"Do you have a specialty?"

"Orthopedic surgeon."

"What does that mean, Doctor?"

"It has to do with the diagnosis and treatment of diseases and deformities of bones and joints and muscles."

Haskell Shapiro asked Dr. McReynolds about the first time he had seen Betty Burke.

"She was in a great deal of pain and emotional tension. I put her in the hospital and put her to bed, and attempted to make her comfortable with the usual medications for pain and muscle spasm, and I put pelvic traction on her to try to relieve her low-back pain. . . . But this didn't relieve her. Really, it made her hurt worse."

Q. This traction and medication and bed rest—over how long a period of time had this been tried, Doctor?

A. Under my care, only the two or three days preceding her surgery.

Q. Generally speaking, what was the purpose of the second operation?

A. To repair a leak in the dural membrane at the lower end of her spinal canal, in the area where we had operated three weeks before, and to remove a collection of spinal fluid and tissue fluid that had formed a cyst in her low back.

Q. Prior to May 2, 1967, did you have any discussions with Betty Burke about the second operation?

A. Well, Betty was seen by Dr. Mooney or me during this period. I was away for a few days' vacation, I believe. The intent of the discussion was that she obviously had a cyst of fluid in her back, and that I thought this should be removed by closing the defect in her dura. At that time she was emotionally quite tense and upset. She was having a lot of headaches. How much actual communication between me and Betty got across, I have no way of knowing, really.

Q. Did you tell her what caused the cyst?

A. I don't know that I told her what caused the cyst, except that I thought it was a leak of spinal fluid, and that we intended to close the leak.

Q. Did you tell her, Doctor, what caused the leak of the spinal fluid?

A. No, I don't know that I discussed the reason why it was leaking.

Deposition of Flora Hoover, R. N., May 20, 1972:

Q. Were you present in the room when Dr. McReynolds discussed the nature of that swelling with Betty Burke?

A. He told her that a second surgery was possible. A few days later he verified that. He told her that it was a—a small leak and would only take a couple of stitches to repair.

Q. Did he say where the leak came from?

A. No, sir. That was his only statement to her.

Q. Did you have any conversations with Dr. McReynolds about your conversations with the patient?

A. Yes, sir. He forbade me to discuss any part of her surgery, because she—because she was too emotional, was the only way he put it to me.

Q. Did you know that the so-called small leak was related to her prior surgery, was a consequence of or resulted from something having to do with the first operation?

A. It's only that during—with our training and all, we— we recognize a few of these things.

Q. In your opinion as a nurse, Mrs. Hoover, did Betty Burke impress you as being emotional?

A. No, sir.

Q. Did she impress you as being an unusual worrier?

A. No, sir.

Q. Did you know that Betty Burke had had a trial concerning an automobile accident of a year or two ago?

A. Yes, I heard about it. She called me on the phone, shortly after the trial.

Q. When she called you did she say anything with reference to these operations?

A. She just said that she was shocked and stunned, that she hadn't known anything about what had really happened to her.

Testimony of Dr. McReynolds, October 2, 1973.
Cross-examination by Harold Hunter:
Q. Did you ever admonish Mrs. Hoover not to discuss with Mrs. Burke the particulars of the aspiration or the repair that you were about to undertake?
A. No. I think I admonished Mrs. Flora Hoover, when Betty was upset, during the time she had the fluid leak from her back, not to discuss that with her because I thought it would be more upsetting to Betty than it was to just change her dressing and take care of her. Because talking to her about it couldn't really change the situation, and it wouldn't make her more calm or more able to accept her situation. . . . Actually it was my privilege, my place to discuss with the patient her problems; it wasn't the nurse's province.

6.

When Haskell Shapiro noticed that the date on the Surgicel brochure he had obtained was 1970, he realized that since Dr. McReynolds had used Surgicel on Betty in 1967, he would have to obtain earlier brochures. It would probably also be useful to have the most up-to-date information available on Surgicel.

He asked David Sabih to write to Johnson and Johnson, the manufacturers of Surgicel, requesting the additional brochures, and copies of several articles and reports concerning Surgicel that were cited in the 1970 brochure.

About a month later, on October 1, Sabih received in the mail the 1970 brochure—which he already had. He wrote again with the same request, and this time received the 1965 brochure, but nothing else.

David Sabih was not a patient man. He dictated the following letter:

October 10, 1973
Dear Mr. Lane:

I have today received from you the brochure of 1965 concerning Surgicel. I also received prior to today a brochure of 1970 regarding Surgicel. But I have not received as yet the brochure for the years in-between 1965 and 1970, nor have I received any brochures which were published regarding Surgicel after 1970. More than a month ago I requested Dr. Schaeffer of Johnson and Johnson to send me copies of articles and reports which are cited in the brochure and which are in the sole possession of Johnson and Johnson. I have yet to receive these articles despite numerous requests.

My client is now totally paralyzed from the waist down. She is paraplegic, and one of the causes of her paraplegia is the use of Surgicel in covering a dural defect. Despite this tragic consequence of the use of Surgicel, Johnson and Johnson callously refuses to furnish us with information regarding the contraindications on the use of Surgicel. Should I not receive from Johnson and Johnson all information that was heretofore requested, within ten days, I shall be forced to file a law suit on behalf of my client to recover all damages resulting from the wrongful conduct of Johnson and Johnson.

I am taking the liberty to enclose a copy of this letter to the president of Johnson and Johnson and also to the officials of the Federal Drug Administration requesting them to conduct an investigation on the uses of Surgicel and regarding the dangers of the use of Surgicel. It is my sincere wish that Johnson and Johnson will comply with our repeated requests so as to avoid legal actions, the loser of which will be Johnson and Johnson.

Very truly yours,
David Sabih

October 10, 1973
Investigative Unit
Federal Drug Administration
Washington, D. C.

Gentlemen:

My client, Betty Burke, is permanently paralyzed from the waist down and is paraplegic. Expert testimony has yielded the following evidence: one of the reasons for her paraplegia is the fact that the surgeon used Surgicel (a product of Johnson and Johnson) to repair a dural defect. The result of such misuse of Surgicel has been the dissolution of Surgicel and its entry into the subarachnoid space.

On numerous occasions, both by writing and by telephone, I have requested further data from Johnson and Johnson regarding their findings on the contraindications on the use of Surgicel. All I have received so far are promises and more promises. It must be concluded that Johnson and Johnson is hiding some important facts from the public, all to their sole economic benefit in peddling Surgicel.

It is submitted that such callous and wrongful conduct should not be condoned, and I urge your agency to conduct a medical investigation into these circumstances.

Very truly yours,
David Sabih

On the 25th of October, Haskell Shapiro received a letter from Johnson and Johnson's attorney:

Dear Mr. Shapiro:

I have, as you know, this date talked with you, and I have also this date forwarded to you certain materials, copies of which I have also forwarded to Mr. Hunter. In my letter to Mr. Hunter, I did not choose to go into the other matters of the conversation, which related strictly to the tactics of your associate, Mr. Sabih.

If Mr. Sabih had made his request to me in the fashion he made it to Johnson and Johnson, I am afraid that my attitude would have been somewhat more belligerent than theirs. Johnson and Johnson have at all times tried to cooperate with everyone but, as you know, it is not always possible to drop one's business for the convenience of someone else.

I can only suggest to Mr. Sabih that, in the future, he do his investigatory work earlier and perhaps avoid some of these problems. I realize the circumstances under which you may have been operating because of your taking over the case from another lawyer at a late moment, but this, in my mind, does not justify sending derogatory material to third parties to the litigation. Johnson and Johnson has cooperated, I believe, to the fullest extent you could ever expect from any third party. The letter to the Food and Drug Administration was, in my opinion, totally uncalled for and completely beyond the bounds of propriety.

It is my understanding that if the present material is adequate for your purposes—which I am sure it will be—that you, personally, will address a letter to the Investigative Unit of the Food and Drug Administration, withdrawing the charges contained in Mr. Sabih's letter of October 10, 1973.

Very truly yours,
G. Edward Fitzgerald
GIBSON, DUNN & CRUTCHER

Upon receipt of the letter and the materials, David Sabih immediately dictated another letter:

October 26, 1973
Dear Mr. Fitzgerald:

I have received your letter dated October 25, 1973, and the enclosed materials from Johnson and Johnson. I believe that your clients have not fully informed you of the true facts concerning this case. Approximately two months ago I contacted Dr. Schaeffer from Johnson and Johnson, requesting him to send to me copies of articles concerning the use of Surgicel, which articles are only in the files of Johnson and Johnson. Dr. Schaeffer promised that he would do so within two days, and he further informed me that Johnson and Johnson files contain a file concerning a case where a patient in New Jersey became paraplegic after a laminectomy due to the use of Surgicel. This information is vital to us since our client, Betty Burke, is also paraplegic after a laminectomy whereby Surgicel was used to repair a dural leak.

Despite the lapse of nearly two months, I have not received any of the above-described materials from Johnson and Johnson. Indeed, all I have received is their brochure. After further telephone calls they still did not provide me with the requested material, and after what I considered to be a very patient waiting period I had no alternative but to inform the Federal Drug Administration of Johnson and Johnson's conduct.

Now I receive from you a package of documents concerning Surgicel. On examination of this package I see copies of brochures which I have already received and which I do not need. None of the articles which deal with Surgicel are enclosed, nor any information provided regarding the patient in New Jersey who became paraplegic after a laminectomy operation and after use of Surgicel. So I am sure that you will forgive me in stating that I do not believe that Johnson and Johnson is cooperating in this matter and that my letter to them was not the result of a spur-of-the-moment thought, but of anxious waiting for two months expecting the fulfillment of unfulfilled promises by a national drug company. So, as matters stand, it is clear at least to me and it would also be clear to you if you do some investigation, that Johnson and Johnson is still not supplying the requested information and that the supply of such information is consistent with good practice of any national and reputable drug company such as your client.

I urge you to urge Johnson and Johnson to supply this

information as soon as possible, since it is material to our case and it may prove of some benefit to other future patients who may avoid permanent harm and injury if all of the contraindications on the use of Surgicel are known.

Sincerely yours,
David Sabih

Dear Mr. Sabih:

In my conversation with you on October 26, you advised me that you would forward to me a specific list of each document that you wanted or each reference to documents. I cannot interpret your letter to constitute such a list and I wish you would provide it to me so that there will be no mistake as to what you want, and no mistake as to what we provide.

Very truly yours,
G. Edward Fitzgerald
GIBSON, DUNN & CRUTCHER

David Sabih sent the detailed list requested, and ultimately received the documents he wanted. He considered subpoenaing Johnson and Johnson, but decided he had enough witnesses without them.

7.

Testimony of Dr. McReynolds, October 1, 1973:

Q. Doctor, isn't it true that you knew on August 12, 1969, that the automobile accident did not cause the arachnoiditis?

A. Well, I am sure that the automobile accident couldn't have caused the arachnoid scar, no. That is true.

Q. Are you making a differentiation between arachnoiditis and the arachnoid scar?

A. No. I am making a differential between the symptoms she had and the presence of the arachnoid scar. She had had the arachnoid scar for a long time—obviously it was a gradual process—but the symptoms which were disabling her at that time dated from just a few days before, at the time of her accident.

Q. All right. Did you tell Betty Burke that her arachnoiditis was not caused by the automobile accident?

A. I don't know that I did. I don't think I did.

Q. Did she tell you that she thought that her problems were from the automobile accident?

A. Historically, yes. She was doing quite well until the automobile accident. Then all of a sudden she was disabled with pain and weakness in her legs which was greatly more than she had had before.

Q. Doctor, did you have any reason, other than historically, as you say, to believe that any of her symptoms or signs or complaints were really due to the automobile accident?

A. No, that is the only data that I had.

Q. Do you recall telling her what caused her arachnoiditis?

A. No, I don't know that I did.

Q. Do you know that you didn't?

A. No, sir. I don't know that I didn't.

Q. Did you ever do anything to dispel her impression that all of her problem derived from the automobile accident?

A. No. She was obviously partially disabled as a result of her initial problem before she ever had this automobile accident.

Q. Did you get the impression, Doctor, from talking to her, that she felt that all of her problems now were as a result of the automobile accident?

A. No.

Q. Did she tell you, Doctor, in words substantially to the effect that she felt that all of her problems were from the automobile accident?

A. Well, so far as she was concerned she was totally disabled suddenly by the result of the automobile accident. But obviously not all of her problems. She knew that not all of her problems arose as a result of the automobile accident.

Q. I am going to read from your deposition of August 14, 1973, page 83:

"She had convinced herself that all of her problems derived from the automobile accident, because she had been getting along pretty good before that, and she got along very badly after that. So that I didn't try to dispel this impression."

"Dr. McReynolds put us to sleep. But we all liked him. He seemed like a very kind person. Most of us agreed that we would not be hesitant about consulting him. He didn't put on a big show, he was very sincere. When Betty Burke went to him in all this pain, I think he felt very sorry for her and was trying to help her in the best way he knew. I think his intentions were of the very best."

—Emma Oaks

"I kinda thought McReynolds was basically a very nice, honest man that made a big mistake. At first I thought he was trying to give an austere, superior impression, and I disliked him. Like, Mr. Sabih would ask him questions and he would look almost disgusted. I don't know if his mannerisms changed or what, but towards the end of the trial I no longer disliked him. He looked very old. I still thought he did wrong, but he was a nice guy that would try to do the right thing."

—Pete Crosetto, juror
aged 30, clerk for U.S. General Accounting Office; law student

"Sometimes Dr. McReynolds did not conduct himself like the person I would have liked him to be. He got upset, he tried to put down the lawyer by what he said to him. That lessened my esteem of Dr. McReynolds as a person. But I still felt that as far as what they were accusing him of, he defended himself well."

—Bob Siemann

Testimony of Dr. McReynolds, October 1, 1973:

Q. Doctor, please tell the Court and the jury what your opinion is as to what it was that caused Betty Burke's arachnoiditis.

A. So far as we are able to know, arachnoiditis is a result of the total of the disrupture insult to the nerve roots, plus the trauma of the surgery and is probably added to by the presence of Pantopaque in the spinal canal which is put in to demonstrate the disrupture before a definitive diagnosis can really be made. The combination of all of these things in people who are susceptible, who are more apt to form scar than other people, produces arachnoiditis.

Q. Are you saying then that in Betty Burke's case it is your opinion that her arachnoiditis was caused by a combination of the things that you mentioned?

A. Yes.

Q. Was there a time you thought otherwise?

A. No, I don't think so.

Q. Doctor, I would like to read from volume 2 of your deposition, page 107:

"She got arachnoiditis from the Pantopaque that Evans left in there originally."

Now, Doctor, in that statement, is it true that you did not say anything about the other causes?

A. No, I didn't. Your question was about the effect of the myelogram.

Q. Now, Doctor, I am going to read from the same volume, page 107:

"It is my opinion that arachnoiditis is a reaction to the Pantopaque. You are the one that keeps bringing up other causes for arachnoiditis. In my opinion the arachnoiditis is more probably a

82

reaction to the presence of Pantopaque regardless of all those other things that happened over and over again. They don't cause arachnoiditis."

Now, Doctor, will you please explain this.

A. Well, I think this is too strong a statement. I was in error in that regard.

Q. Doctor, would you please explain the difference now in your opinion.

A. Well, I don't think I ride quite as hard on Pantopaque as I did at that time.

Q. Beg your pardon?

A. I don't think I ride quite as hard on Pantopaque. Yeah, I should think I changed my opinion somewhat. As I think about it a little bit, I think these other things are taken into consideration.

Q. But six weeks ago, you felt that it was the Pantopaque dye that caused it?

A. At that time, that particular time when you were questioning me, yes.

8.

One of the specialists who agreed to testify on Betty's behalf was Dr. William Hellerstein, a well-known neurosurgeon. He examined her, was paid an expert witness fee of $1,300, and then indicated to Haskell Shapiro that he had changed his mind: he would not testify.

Although Haskell knew that Dr. Hellerstein often testified for the defense in malpractice cases, he was mystified by this sudden about-face. He decided to go to see the doctor, and to carry a small tape recorder in his pocket. He might be able to record the facts behind the doctor's change of mind.

He looked all over town for a tape recorder small enough to be kept in a coat pocket. When he finally found one, he telephoned Dr. Hellerstein to make an appointment. He was curious about the doctor's decision not to testify, he said, and wondered if they could get together and discuss it.

"Certainly," said the doctor. "I'll be glad to talk to you about it. Oh, and by the way—be sure to bring a tape recorder."

What Dr. Hellerstein told Haskell was that he had decided his testimony would hurt rather than help Betty's case, since he now felt that there had been no malpractice.

9.

Another of the expert witnesses David Sabih located was Dr. R. Van Houten, an eminent neurosurgeon who had performed about a thousand laminectomy operations. He testified on Friday, September 28. Later on the same day, the plaintiff's attorneys were informed by the defendants' attorneys that the defendants intended to move for a mistrial. This motion was based on Dr. Van Houten's statement in his testimony that some of the medical malpractice claims against him had been paid by an insurance carrier. The defendants claimed that such mention before the jury was prejudicial—that is, knowing Dr. Van Houten had been protected by insurance would lead the jury to assume the current defendants were similarly protected. This assumption might incline the jury to decide in the plaintiff's favor. It is, of course, common knowledge that doctors protect themselves against malpractice claims by paying large insurance premiums; the jurors needed only commonsense to tell them the defendants in their case were insured. But law and commonsense do not always agree.

The plaintiff's attorneys submitted to the court an opposition to the motion, contending that the move for a mistrial was without merit.

"Defendants' counsel is a distinguished and eminent medical malpractice lawyer," it began. "Indeed, he is the senior partner of a distinguished law firm which specializes in medical malpractice defense. Defendants' counsel conducted what may be considered a thorough, complete and brilliant cross-examination of Dr. Van Houten. Indeed, the examination was so thorough that it elicited points which may be considered irrelevant and immaterial to this lawsuit. Nevertheless, it was apparent that defendants' counsel determined that a thorough cross-examination was required, and an effort to impeach the character and testimony of Dr. Van Houten was embarked upon."

In his cross-examination, Harold Hunter had questioned Dr. Van Houten in detail about various articles Dr. Van Houten had written in fields other than his specialty:

Q. Doctor, you wrote an article, "Virus-like Bodies in Human Breast Cancer." Are you an internal medicine specialist?

A. No. I was doing cancer research at the time and that was part of my project.

Q. How about your article, "Selection of Blood Donors"? How does that relate to neurology?

A. Same thing. We were endeavoring to encourage better selection of blood donors and to cut out the so-called Skid Row donor and prevent the hepatitis and the danger of transmission of diseases.

Q. How about the article in 1954 entitled, "Doctor, Are You Anemic"?

A. Well, this was while I was working as editor of the *Life and Health* magazine. It is a general doctors' magazine, not particularly having to do with my specialty.

Q. On what authority did you write the article, "The Surgical Management of Chronic Ulcerative Colitis"?

A. This is a very outstanding paper for which I have had requests from all over the world. I wrote this particular paper as part of my Master's degree from the University of Michigan. It was part of my general surgical training in which I later qualified for the American Board of Surgery.

Q. Were you pursuing the specialty of gastro-enteritis when you wrote your article on diverticulosis of the colon?

A. It is a part of neurosurgical training to take some general surgery, so I wrote the paper during that time.

Q. Are you likewise a specialist on anesthesia? I think you wrote "Anesthesia and Analgesia"?

A. I don't think I was the principal author of that article, it was simply an article written with the anesthesiology department.

Q. How about the article "Why Some Doctors Take Dope"? Was that equally outstanding?

A. Well, Counsel, I don't think that is appropriate.

Q. Excuse me. Was it equally well-received then, Doctor?

A. Yes.

It was obvious to everyone that the purpose of this line of questioning was to discredit Dr. Van Houten by showing that he had published articles in fields in which he was not a recognized authority. However, it probably served only to indicate to the jury the breadth of Dr. Van Houten's medical knowledge. Harold Hunter was more successful in his attempts to discredit Dr. Van Houten when he questioned him as to the problems he had had with various hospitals—problems which Dr. Van Houten described as "political": his operating privileges had been restricted in three Glendale hospitals, so that in order to operate in those hospitals he had to be accompanied by another neurosurgeon.

When Harold Hunter got to the matter of the malpractice claims against Dr. Van Houten, the statement of the plaintiff's attorneys continued, he "elicited the response of Dr. Van Houten that some of these cases against him were with merit and some without merit, and that in those which had merit, he arranged to pay the injured patients and such payment was made by the insurance carrier. At no time did defendants ever object to this line of answers. . . . Dr. Van Houten made the statement that when he thought the claims against him were just, he wanted justice done to his patients, and arranged for

86

payment. It is probable that defendants decided that such a statement is very detrimental to their case . . . and now they want the court to help them cover up their error. . . . If defendants are truly interested in justice in this case, they might heed the words of Dr. Van Houten and do justice to this permanently and totally disabled plaintiff.

"The court can take judicial notice that the entire cost of the defense is not being paid by defendants but by an insurance company. The fees charged by defendants' counsel are paid by an insurance company on a per diem time basis. No wonder it is of no consequence to defendants nor to their attorneys to require another trial, since none of these expenses will have to be borne by them. . . . Plaintiff is not in the same enviable position. Plaintiff has already incurred a medical bill for over $20,000 at Orange County Rehabilitation Center. . . . It is submitted that plaintiff should not be subjected to any further injustice by requiring plaintiff to go through the agony of this trial one more time due to errors committed by defendants."

Nothing came of the defendants' motion for a mistrial.

10.

"Of course, Wallace Reed, who was handling the case before I came into it, gave me the impression that the gravity of the case spoke for itself. The serious nature of the injuries gave me reason to anticipate an inevitable sympathy factor. Nevertheless, my own evaluation, based on a thorough study of all the records, and the apparent disdain of Mr. Halprin, who had once been the plaintiff's attorney, for the case, suggested to me a good chance for the defense.

"As the trial progressed, my hopes were enhanced by several factors. First, the plaintiff called as one of their witnesses Dr. Van Houten, who had a history of substantial malpractice litigation against him. In addition, his surgical operating privileges had been somewhat curtailed in two or three hospitals in Glendale. Second, I had several highly qualified experts who were willing to testify for the defense. And third, the relative inexperience of my opposition: Mr. Shapiro had not had too much experience in medical malpractice, and Mr. Sabih was trying his first malpractice case, possibly his first superior court jury case. While they were both extremely tenacious from beginning to end, and highly sincere, they were not always as smooth as experienced malpractice counsel. I felt I had an edge in courtroom competency."

—Harold Hunter

11.

One of the spectators in the courtroom was making sketches of the witnesses and the members of the jury. When Judge McGinley noticed it, he confiscated the sketches and ordered the artist to make no more.

Betty Burke's sister-in-law, her brother Everett's wife, came to the courtroom every day and took copious notes on the proceedings to relay to Betty, who was still in the Rehabilitation Center. One day she asked the judge if she could bring a tape recorder to court to save her the trouble of taking all those notes. The judge refused.

"Adverse to Betty Burke was the fact that members of her family testified and were conspicuous in their presence throughout the trial. The impression may have been given to the jury that they had more than a passing interest in any recovery she might obtain."

—Harold Hunter

12.

"Spindle? The first time he spoke, if I'd based my opinion on the way he acted, he would've been out the door right then. I really tried to put aside the way he presented himself, but as far as appearance went, that man wouldn't touch me with a ten-foot pole."

—Roseann Halte, juror
aged 20, billing clerk

"None of us went by our personal feelings. If you use your feelings as a reason for doing someone in, that's really bad. But he sure didn't win us over. He's a very arrogant man. Maybe he can't help it, or maybe he has reason to be. But he was very sure of himself, and in a case like that it just didn't seem very good. . . . Maybe he thought a little humor would make everyone think he was a real jolly fellow; but it wasn't the time or place as far as we were concerned. We didn't think it was funny at all. He might have been told something about it, because the next time he appeared he was much more subdued.

"The 'Fat Jesus' business shocked us, every one of us. I think if it had been me, I'd have gotten up out of bed and walked out."

—Emma Oaks

"Dr. Spindle probably gave the most negative impression of anybody that testified. He seemed very phony, like a very scared, nervous man who was trying to give the impression of pooh-poohing the whole thing. He said he felt this was the greatest personal triumph he'd ever had in his history of being a doctor. I mean, here's a woman who's totally paralyzed! He seemed insensitive to the whole thing.

"I guess that by 'great personal triumph,' he was saying, I

89

took a woman that could not walk, and I made her walk. And after each of the operations he performed, she did improve for a little amount of time, particularly after his second operation, when it had been predicted by both Spindle and McReynolds that she'd never walk again, and she did walk. I think she cooked Thanksgiving dinner at one point. When he removed the scar tissue from the nerves, it would take a certain amount of time for it to grow back again. After the initial shock, when the nerves would start to function, she'd get her feeling back. And apparently out of pure blind luck, or the grace of God, or both, he did a good enough job on the second operation so that she did start to walk again. But once the scar tissue did start to form again, it was more rapid than it had been before."

—Pete Crosetto

"I have to admit that I didn't care much for Dr. Spindle. He just struck me bad. I wouldn't let him touch my dog, and I don't care much for my dog."

—Bob Siemann

"He acted smart-alecky."

—Dolores Loya, juror
aged 45, housewife

"I did not respect him as a doctor, particularly. It seemed that he didn't really feel he should be on trial—he seemed to be saying that he was the doctor, and who were we, twelve laymen, to judge him?"

—Verla Holloway, juror
aged 47, housewife

Dr. David Kent Spindle testified for the first time on October 3. One of the first questions Haskell Shapiro asked him was whether he was Board certified.

"No, I am not."

"Have you taken the examination to become Board certified?"

"Twice."

"And you have failed it each time?"

"Yes, I have."

"When were those two times?"

"I don't even remember."

Harold Hunter, when he cross-examined Dr. Spindle, elicited the information that Dr. Spindle enjoyed unrestricted staff privileges at a number of local hospitals, had been Chief of Staff at Downey Community Hospital, and had taught neural surgery at Loma Linda University.

"Apparently it's not required to be Board certified, and apparently there are a good many doctors who other professional people feel are competent, who are not Board certified. It would matter to me, if I were the one seeking service. But apparently, to Betty Burke it didn't matter. If it mattered, she should have asked. I think I would ask . . . now. At that time, I don't think I would've. But then I think that those are the risks we encounter in living. Now, if there was a law that a doctor has to say 'I'm not Board certified,' and he doesn't say it, then he's negligent. Until there is such a law, he's not negligent."

—Bob Siemann

In his testimony, Dr. Spindle explained that the dural sac has three membranes covering the brain and spinal cord:

"You can remember them by mnemonics, from inside out: pia, arachnoid, dura, and it spells PAD. Usually doctors use dirty limericks, but this isn't too bad. So you can remember. You didn't know that, did you? Okay. . . .

"Now, the fluid travels between the pia and the arachnoid. The outside is the hard layer or the dura mater. Now, just a point of interest, the way it got its name is that they were the original hippies. That really means 'hard mother.' Dura mater, that is, hard mother."

Haskell Shapiro asked him if it was reasonable to expect scar tissue and adhesions to come back, worse than before, after an operation to remove them.

"No . . . it is not true that just because you go in and operate that you are going to have more and more scarring."

Haskell then read from Dr. Spindle's testimony at the auto accident trial in July, 1971:

Q. Now, in addition to the findings of your operation of August, 1969, you were aware that there was a great probability that they would recur after your surgery, isn't that true?

A. Yes, after my original surgery.

Q. Unfortunately, once this condition is prevalent in a person there is very little a doctor can do to avoid it, isn't that true?

A. Well, it is usually chronically progressive, that is correct, sir.

He asked Dr. Spindle if he was still of the same opinion.

A. It was my opinion then, it is my opinion now. It's a bad, bad illness. And some cases you can help, and in those you are eternally grateful and they are eternally grateful. But you must view each case with pessimism.

Q. Well, as a matter of fact, was Betty not very much worse after your operation, about a year after, in November of 1970?

A. Counselor, Betty Burke was immediately relieved from her condition. I was delighted. Unfortunately, a year later, as you suggested, she had chronic progression of her illness.

Q. The immediate result was excellent, but the long-range result was very bad, is that correct?

A. I think the long-range result from both surgeries and everything that's happened to Betty has been dismal. I wish to God it hadn't been. I wish I could have stemmed it, and I hope we will be able to stem it in others.

Q. I am sure that is your feeling, Doctor.

Later, Haskell Shapiro questioned Dr. Spindle about the tube he had put in Betty's spine during the fourth operation:

Q. Tell us about this tube, Doctor, that you used. You say that it is used often as a substitute for dura?

A. Yes. If we put on a dural patch or we open the dura and we don't have enough dura to close it with, we will use dural substitute. I use it routinely. I have used it this week.

Q. Had you put the Silastic tubes in before?

A. No, sir.

Q. This was the first time that you ever did that?

A. The first time I ever fastened Silastic in this fashion.

Q. Had you heard of its being done before?

A. No, sir, never heard of it being done before. Everything you do in brain surgery, which is neurosurgery, I never know what I am going to do in the next case. That is what makes it exciting because there are so many variables that you meet. You have to be careful to work with known materials, materials that have been tested.

I would like to put this issue to rest. It is not unlike the lady working with the dress material and she does a different tuck in the dress than she ever did before and she hopes it turns out good, and sometimes it does, and other times it looks like a terrible tuck.

Q. Had you ever discussed this procedure with any of your colleagues before you did it?

A. No. I told them afterwards, and they thought it was an interesting idea.

Q. Is it possible that the presence of this tube itself could cause any problems?

A. Absolutely not, absolutely not. It is a completely inert material. We put it on the brain. It is like a very thin rubbery membrane and very easily compressible, and I had hoped that it would be a conduit.

Q. All right. I will represent to you, Doctor, that there was a physician, a Dr. Van Houten, who testified that in his opinion Betty would have to undergo another operation to have this tube removed. Would you disagree with that?

A. Most violently.

Q. Do you feel that it is possible that this tube could cause any pressure?

A. No. It did not cause—it is not causing her any pressure.

Dr. Spindle inserted this Teflon insert in my back, which was an experimental thing—I knew nothing about it, signed nothing. We found out later that this had been done exactly three times in the United States. I guess at this point they had gotten desperate, they were willing to try anything because they had really gotten in over their heads. But you just don't experiment on people without telling them.

13.

Shortly after the trial began, David Sabih made arrangements to go to the Orange County Rehabilitation Center and make a film, to be called "A Day in the Life of Betty Burke." He spent an entire day there, and eventually wound up with about three hours of film that he planned to use at the trial.

When he indicated his intention to introduce the film as evidence, the defense objected strenuously. Judge McGinley agreed to view the film himself and decide whether or not it was admissible.

After seeing it, the judge ruled that certain portions of it were too "inflammatory" for use. He allowed the showing of approximately one third of the original film.

As shown in the courtroom, the film record of a day in Betty's life in the Rehabilitation Center began at 7:00 A.M. It showed Betty applying make-up, getting off the bed and into the wheelchair, and eating breakfast. She filled out the day's menu for herself and the woman in the next bed; she took her pills and medications. Next was a shower: two nurses wrapped her in a net and brought her to the shower, which had a specially installed chair. Then they took her from the shower, helped her dry herself, brought her back to the ward and flipped her from the net into bed.

Getting dressed was a struggle; a nurse had to put her socks on for her. Later in the morning, more medication; then an attendant put her into a truck for the trip to the physical therapy room. There, with the aid of braces, a walker, and a therapist, she "walked" six feet.

After lunch, she sat by the telephone to take messages for the Center. She took a nap; her mother and brother visited. More medications; then dinner.

"The plaintiff's counsel left no stone unturned. They prepared a videotape on a day in the life of Betty Burke—it showed her activities, ranging from the painful move from the wheelchair to the bed, to meals, being taken to the shower, physical therapy. It caused a profound sympathy reaction."

—Harold Hunter

14.

One of the major elements of the plaintiff's case was the use of Surgicel to close a dural defect. Dr. McReynolds stated on the witness stand that "it had been our custom for several years that if there is some oozing in the laminectomy defect at the time we are ready to close the wound, we take a patch of Surgicel and just lay it over the hole where the muscles would come down against the surface of it so the wound shuts." Haskell Shapiro had been looking forward to questioning Dr. McReynolds about the Surgicel:

Q. Isn't it true, Doctor, that Surgicel is effective only in the presence of whole blood?

A. Right.

Q. Isn't it also true, Doctor, that there was spinal fluid that was leaking from the spinal canal through that opening you had created in the dura?

A. Yes.

Q. Isn't it true that there is a likelihood of that Surgicel becoming saturated with spinal fluid which is leaking from the spinal canal?

A. I am sure that's true.

Q. And then in that case, Doctor, isn't it true that the Surgicel would not be in the presence of whole blood by the time the blood on the other side came in contact with the Surgicel?

A. Would you please read back the question? I am not sure I followed the exact wording.

Q. Yes. Isn't it true that the Surgicel, having been saturated or come into contact with the spinal fluid, would no longer—it could no longer be said that it was in the presence of whole blood, isn't that true, Doctor?

A. No, that's not true. As soon as the wound tissues were pushed together and closed down on the surface of the dura, whole blood was there where the Surgicel lay on the surface of the dura.

. . . . .

Q. This spinal fluid which was leaking—does it have any clotting ability?

A. No.

Q. As a matter of fact, it is about 98½ per cent water, is that correct?

A. At least that.

Q. If that mixes with blood, is that mixture whole blood?

A. No. It is a diluted solution of whole blood and spinal fluid.

Q. Isn't that what we have here on the outside of the Surgicel—whole blood coming in contact with this diluted material—that is, the dilutant?

A. No. Yes. I think so.

On September 28, Dr. Van Houten testified that hemostasis (clotting) would not occur in the presence of a leak of spinal fluid. "The spinal fluid would, of course, dilute any blood, so the platelets could not get to the Surgicel to produce a clot and do any sealing."

On October 1, Haskell Shapiro again questioned Dr. McReynolds about Surgicel:

Q. I believe you testified the other day that in order for Surgicel to be effective it must be in the presence of whole blood; is that correct?

A. Yes, that is correct.

Q. And if the Surgicel becomes saturated with spinal fluid, is it not true then that the Surgicel could not be expected to be effective?

A. Not until blood fills the fibers or between the fibers of the Surgicel.

Q. You are saying then that after it is wet with the spinal fluid it could still be expected to be effective because of blood coming to it?

A. Yes. With a raw bloody surface, applied right to the surface of the Surgicel, I expect it to clot.

Q. Actually, Doctor, isn't it true that you did not know whether the Surgicel would stop the leak?

A. Obviously it didn't.

Q. I know that. But I am saying isn't it true that you did not know whether it would?

A. Your question doesn't make sense. I expected it to and it didn't. What else is there to say?

. . . . .

Q. Last Tuesday, Doctor, you testified that it has been your custom for several years to use Surgicel, is that correct?

A. That's correct.

Q. And has it been your custom for the last few years to place Surgicel over the dura to stop a dural leak?

A. No, I haven't had dural leaks to stop with Surgicel. You put Surgicel over the exposed surface of the dura before closing the wound very frequently just as a matter of separating the dural surface from the muscle surface that overlies it.

But no, it's not our custom to treat dural leaks with

97

Surgicel. We don't have that many dural leaks. When you have one, if the hole is big enough we sew it shut. If it's a tiny puncture hole we close the wound with the expectation that the normal process of blood clot will seal the hole.

Q. Then, Doctor, is it your testimony that normally you do not use Surgicel to close a dural leak?

A. Counselor, this one occasion was the only time in my experience when I have used it. It's not my custom.

Q. Can you tell us why it is that this is the only time that you ever used Surgicel for the purpose of stopping a dural leak?

A. No, I don't know that I have any answer to that question.

On October 9, Dr. Frederic Pitts testified that Surgicel was known to be an irritating substance and was not generally used to plug holes in the dura or in situations where one was not trying to stop bleeding. "Usually if you have a hole in the dura, you sew it up or put a patch of something else over it."

On October 3, Dr. Spindle was asked about the use of Surgicel for patching a dural leak:

A. I am not sure it's worth a tinker's damn. I use it. It's used to stop blood. I am not so sure that I don't put it on because of habit. But I have no firm opinion whether it would help, or close a dural leak. It makes some sense to form a little pressure backwards by any inert object that's not going to cause any problems. But as far as stopping dural leaks, I am not sure it's worth anything.

Q. Is that because it should be used only in the presence of whole blood?

A. This has been belabored. The whole blood refers to all of the elements of the blood being there, and not just the serum. The Surgicel is effective for stopping bleeding even in diluted whole blood.

Q. Doctor, what is diluted whole blood?

A. Well, it doesn't have any of the formed elements removed. In other words, it hasn't had the plasma, the red cells or the various blood constituents removed. When we speak of whole blood what we really mean in medicine is that it is not fractionated blood.

Q. If the Surgicel becomes saturated with spinal fluid will it then be likely to be effective?

A. I have already said I don't know whether it is effective or not. I really suspicion that the only reason I use it is that some surgeons like neat and tidy things and it's nice and white. It may sound silly, but that's the honest truth.

15.

It is not news that medical malpractice insurance rates have soared in recent years. In California, rates for orthopedic surgeons, for example (one of the specialties considered "high-risk"), rose from $480 annually in 1958 to about $14,000 in 1975. A further increase of 400% in early 1976 led to a work slowdown in some areas of the state. Many physicians were forced to move to other states where malpractice insurance rates are lower. Others left the field of medicine altogether, either for another career or for early retirement. Most, however, eventually knuckled under and paid.

These sky-high insurance rates (which are, of course, ultimately passed on to the patients in the form of higher fees for medical care) might lead one to assume that a considerable proportion of patients who are unhappy with the results of their treatment sue their doctors. This is not the case. In 1970, for instance, the ratio of malpractice claims to doctor visits was one in a quarter-million. Of approximately six million cases of injury resulting from poor medical or surgical care in 1974, only twenty thousand—or one in every three hundred—generated a malpractice claim. And of these, less than half were settled in the patient's favor.

Of those cases which the patients win, very few receive the giant awards that make headlines. The Commission on Medical Malpractice, organized by the Secretary of Health, Education and Welfare, found that only one-fourth of the malpractice suits settled in 1970 brought awards of more than $10,000, and that only 3% brought $100,000 or more.

It is true, however, that the number of malpractice claims is increasing, as are the amounts of money awarded to successful plaintiffs. In the history of the state of California up to 1975, for instance, only sixteen cases had been settled for $1,000,000 or more, but most of these had occurred between 1973 and 1975, and such awards are now averaging about one a month.

Lest anyone think that patients' high medical fees go back to them in the form of malpractice settlements, figures released by the Department of Health, Education and Welfare indicate a large discrepancy between amounts paid in insurance premiums and amounts received by injured patients. Of every dollar that doctors pay in premiums, patients receive less than twenty cents in awards. Thirty-one cents goes for insurance sales and investigatory and administrative costs. Forty cents goes to defense lawyers, and ten to fifteen cents to plaintiffs' lawyers.

The growth of large malpractice suits has led doctors to practice what they call "defensive medicine": such things as extra consultations, extra (and sometimes unnecessary) tests, hospitalizations, follow-ups—all of which add to medical costs and guarantee the doctor a good defense if he or she should be sued. This extra vigilance may result in benefit to the patient. On the other hand, a new, experimental treatment or test, which might benefit the patient, may be rejected because it entails risks to the patient, and thus the risk of a malpractice claim against the doctor.

Some doctors, blaming the malpractice crisis on ambulance-chasing lawyers, have proposed no-fault malpractice insurance similar to no-fault automobile liability insurance. Others want a commission established that would limit damages, as

100

with workmen's compensation, to a specific schedule. Such a commission would evaluate each case, recommend awards to pay for actual costs and losses and provide appropriate income, and send to a separate investigative panel any evidence of negligence.

Still other physicians would like to see the contingency legal-fee system eliminated. Under this system, if a lawyer accepts a case and loses, the plaintiff owes him nothing; if he wins or the case is settled out of court, the lawyer is entitled to between 30% and 50% of the award. The physicians claim that the system encourages patients to press doubtful claims, since they have nothing to lose. But the contingency system discourages attorneys from accepting cases that do not appear to have a good chance, since they must expend time and money on the preparation of the case; and elimination of the system would make it difficult or impossible for the poor to sue. In the case of Betty Burke, Haskell Shapiro had disbursed some $60,000 on behalf of his client by the time the trial ended. Defense attorneys take no such chance: win or lose, they are paid by their client's insurance company.

16.

At the center of the plaintiff's case was the contention that Dr. McReynolds had been negligent in failing to suture the dural defect he had created (by whatever means; the defendants claimed it was made with a needle in order to remove excess Pantopaque dye) during the first surgery. His handwritten report, made shortly after the operation, said nothing about removal of dye; but the formal typed report, made later and in greater detail, indicated that he had inserted a 20-gauge needle and removed two to three cc. of dye.

Haskell Shapiro questioned Dr. McReynolds about this difference between the two reports:

Q. Dr. McReynolds, would you make your records in handwriting and then have it typed afterwards?

A. No. I would make it in handwriting, right at the time immediately following the surgery, and would dictate it, which would later be transcribed by the secretary.

Q. So would you usually tend to make your handwritten notes pretty complete?

A. No, I think not including all the technical details, for instance, of an operation. But I would make my handwritten note to include what I thought was most significant.

Q. Doctor, was it significant in the first operation on April 10, 1967, that you decided to remove the Pantopaque material from Betty's spine?

A. Yes, I thought so . . .

Q. Now, there is nothing in your handwritten notes about removing any Pantopaque dye from the spinal column, is there?

A. No, that was included in the dictated note.

Q. And there was nothing in there about any minimal spinal fluid leak, was there?

A. No.

Q. There was nothing in there about the small patch of Surgicel?

A. No.

The doctor's hand slips; he makes a nick in the dura; he decides to say nothing. Later, when the continued leak of spinal fluid and the formation of a cyst make a second operation essential, he has to account for the dural defect which it is now obvious he created. He dictates a report of the first surgery, in which he says he inserted a needle to remove Pantopaque dye.

Did it happen this way?

17.

A doctor and some nurses who had treated Betty at the Orange County Rehabilitation Center testified to her constant pain, her anguish during the first weeks at the Center when she had involuntarily soiled her bed or clothes because of her lack of bladder and bowel control, the problems involved in simple tasks like taking a shower. There were recurrent decubiti, or sores, from the pressure of the wheelchair. Bladder infections are a common problem for paraplegics; she had already had several and would probably have more. She would probably require drugs for the rest of her life. She had been at the Center since March of 1973—seven months, at a charge of approximately $100 per day.

I was scared of going back into a hospital. But that didn't last long. The people there were some of the most fantastic people in the world. There were all kinds of disabilities—people who'd had strokes, paraplegics, quadriplegics—and so much compassion among them, it got so I spent more time thinking about other people than I did worrying about myself. They know exactly how you feel when you come in, full of anxiety and fear; they put you right at ease. You don't feel like an oddball, because everyone is handicapped. We still keep in touch, I visit them and many have visited me.

The rehabilitation is mostly physical. The mental is left mostly up to the other patients. A few of 'em had to have shrinks, though. But there's committees, and the patients help each other. One patient can get through to another often where a doctor or nurse couldn't.

Therapy was in the morning. You put on braces that come to the waist, and get into a walker—so at least you get your kidneys in the right position. You roll the walker and your legs move along, maybe about six feet and then back. Then they lay you on a table and bend your legs to your chest, move your feet around to keep the circulation going. You work with your arms to strengthen the muscles. Twice a day they lower you into a tank of medicated water, a whirlpool bath. There was about three or four hours a day of therapy.

Sometimes we'd have lunch at the table to get the patients to socialize, because many of them would withdraw from life. At night there were bingo games, television, movies, sometimes movies the patients had made themselves. We had quite a few people from other countries, France and Germany—and they'd bring in movies from their countries for them.

As you progress, you're allowed to go home weekends.

I was in a ward of eighteen beds. Curtains were the only privacy. That bothered me a great deal at first, but if I ever had to go back I wouldn't have it any other way. Being so close, there were times when patients actually saved each other's lives, realizing something was wrong and ringing for the nurse.

18.

Haskell Shapiro and David Sabih thought it might help Betty's case to have Dr. John M. Suarez, a psychiatrist, do an evaluation to determine how much psychological damage had been caused by her condition and whether or not she would require psychotherapy. Dr. Suarez reported that Betty talked about her condition "in a very bland way. . . . She talks about the fact that one cannot ever totally adjust to such a situation and that one always retains a measure of hope. She denies that she is significantly depressed . . . brags about being always active and independent. . . . There has been discussion of several further surgical procedures, but she is reluctant to undergo anything else. . . .

"She relies heavily on the mechanism of isolation, that is, the absence of an emotional component when describing typically difficult issues. Her entire narrative is full of examples of the mechanism of denial, pertaining to both her despair and depression and also to her anger, which is thinly veiled and just below the surface. . . . The patient is suffering from a depression of at least moderate severity. Such a reaction is expected and inevitable under the circumstances. The main problem lies in how she is coping with it. Instead of facing the situation squarely and working through the losses emotionally, which is a healthy response in order to achieve adjustment, she is handling it primarily through the mechanism of denial. . . . The pathological aspect of denial lies in the fact that dealing with reality is postponed, and thus the process of readjustment is also put off."

In a case conference at the Rehabilitation Center, Betty had been asked what she would choose if a miracle were possible. She had replied that it was a toss-up between getting rid of her pain or resuming her sexual activities. She told Dr. Suarez that this reply had been criticized, because "the 'right' response was to be able to walk again."

"She attempts to rationalize her 'wrong' response," Dr. Suarez reported, "by saying that without pain and with special equipment she could function well."

In cross-examination on the witness stand, Harold Hunter asked if Dr. Suarez would agree with the characterization of Betty by several witnesses as courageous, with a strong mental composition.

"No. I think that description applies to her activities and her outward demeanor. I feel that I have some insight into what is going on below the surface."

Did Dr. Suarez agree that Betty endeavored to be cheerful in spite of her misfortunes?

"Yes."

And that she took pleasure in trying to encourage and help and cheer others who had had similar misfortunes?

"Yes."

And that she liked to help to the limited physical extent she could, by answering telephones and doing other things of a helpful nature?

"Yes."

"Are these not positive, encouraging characteristics in a person who has the gross misfortune that Betty Burke has?"

"They may or may not be. They have to be taken in context for them to be interpreted properly."

"Do they not show an ability on her part to think positively rather than negatively?"

"At a superficial level, yes."

"But you have the capability of going deeper; is that right, sir?"

"I have the capability of understanding the total picture beyond what is on the surface, yes."

Among the psychological tests which had been administered to Betty were the Sentence Completion Test, the Thematic Apperception Test, the Rorschach ink-blot test, and the Minnesota Multiphasic Personality Inventory. The latter consists of several hundred true-or-false questions, such as, "I love my mother"; "I like science"; "It is not hard for me to ask help from my friends even though I cannot return the favor." The answers are scored by "a rather elaborate process," according to Dr. Suarez, and the scores are translated onto a profile sheet, one side of which is used for males, the other for females. According to the test, the answers that would characterize a healthy male are not the same as those that would characterize a healthy female.

Dr. Louise Epps, a clinical psychologist, had also interviewed Betty. She had reported that Betty "has reacted to her disability . . . mainly by denying the seriousness and the permanence of the condition" and "still desperately clings to the fantasy that with recent developments in medicine she will one day regain her ability to walk." She agreed with Dr. Suarez that Betty "defends herself from painful depressive feelings by marked use of denial. She denies any suicidal thoughts . . . manifests restlessness and attempts to over-involve herself in what activities are available to her. . . . Suffers from a marked disturbance in body image. Mrs. Burke harbors many fantasies concerning bodily mutilation and disfigurement. She perceives herself as having a disfigured and destroyed body."

Dr. Epps had concluded that Betty was "moderately emotionally withdrawn. She has probably had a history of rather stormy and transient interpersonal relationships in which she has avoided realizing true intimacy. While she says that she is very close to and loves other people, especially her stepsons, her real affectional ties tend to be rather shallow and ambivalent."

Dr. Suarez felt that Betty did indeed need therapy, which "would be aimed primarily at providing the additional support needed to help her to acknowledge her feelings and to begin to digest her predicament. By necessity, this will have to be gradual, for stripping her of her defenses abruptly and without providing an alternative would trigger a massive depression with the distinct risk of suicide."

Did Dr. Suarez think it would be better, Harold Hunter asked, if Betty did not indulge in activity?

"I would say it is important for her to engage in activities to begin to find alternatives and different ways of adjusting."

"Isn't this precisely what she is doing?"

"No, and that is where the problem lies. She is doing this not as a way of adjusting and finding a new life, but rather as a way of keeping herself so occupied with external things that she doesn't allow herself the time or the energy to deal with what is happening with her."

"Doctor, gratefully and thankfully, you and I have not been in the position Betty Burke is in, but I suggest to you that there are two ways to go: one can either wallow in self-pity or one can pursue activities, as Betty Burke appears to be doing. Is it your suggestion that she stop these activities and simply give up?"

Those were both pathological ways, Dr. Suarez replied. There was a third way, "the healthiest way: to begin to accept gradually her predicament and deal with the feelings that accompany that situation rather than repressing them or making believe that they are not there . . . the activities in themselves are not harmful. The problem comes in how she is using them psychologically . . ."

Harold Hunter was having considerable difficulty in concealing his contempt for Dr. Suarez's theories. "Whether you are a psychiatrist, orthopedist, lawyer, I don't care what specialty you pursue, you must agree with me that it has got to be therapeutic and helpful when one person can cheer another person up and make him feel a little better. Would you agree with that?"

"No, not necessarily. . . . An example that comes to mind would be a manic patient who stands on a crowded corner of downtown Los Angeles and gives out $5 bills to the passersby. Now, that is a kindly gesture. I am sure it is welcome and accepted by the recipients, but for that patient, the actions are a symptom or a manifestation of some serious problems within him, and therefore in that instance I could not consider his actions as therapeutic to him."

"Are you troubled by the premise that perhaps this very day, in ignorance of what you are telling us here, Betty Burke is perhaps right now helping somebody, trying to make their day a little easier for them? Does that bother you as a physician?"

"Not at all. The fact that she is helping others for the sake of others is welcome to me. I am concerned about the fact that she is not really helping herself."

The shrinks in Rehab always wanted to know if I'd had thoughts of suicide. When I said no, they said, Never? No, never, I said. They said, Why not? I said, What kind of a question is that? They acted like that just wasn't normal.

19.

On October 8, the Pacific Indemnity Group, which insured the defendants, offered to settle the case for $150,000.

Betty already owed the Orange County Rehabilitation Center some $22,000. Haskell Shapiro had already advanced about $30,000 for the costs of the case. Betty would receive less than $100,000 from the settlement, of which her attorneys would get 50%, as was customary under the contingency fee system in California. In addition, she would lose the opportunity to have her medical bills paid by Medicare and Medi-Cal and to obtain welfare benefits.

David Sabih wrote to the insurance company that "As matters stand now it would be extremely disadvantageous to her to accept your offer. I know that both parties are subjected to a cruel dilemma. . . . The insurance company placed an initial evaluation on this case in the amount of $10,000, and I appreciate the psychological barrier that this entails, especially when the same appraiser has to go to the same insurance company and say that the case he evaluated at the $10,000 level is now worth more than $150,000."

20.

How big was the "dural defect" that Dr. McReynolds created during the first operation, the defect that continued to leak spinal fluid for three weeks, forming a cyst and making a second operation necessary? Was it of sufficient size to have warranted suturing?

"As I remember, it was about 3/16 of an inch," Dr. McReynolds testified on September 25. If it had been as much as half an inch long, he said, he certainly would have sutured it.

On October 1, Haskell Shapiro asked Dr. McReynolds how many stitches he had used to suture the defect when he went back in for the second operation.

"Four of them."

"How far apart were the four stitches?"

"They are placed very close together. About 3/32 of an inch apart."

"Then how far would it be from the first suture to the fourth suture?"

"About 9/32 of an inch."

Was he certain that the intervals could not have been 4/32?

"4/32 would be 1/8 of an inch apart. No, I am sure they are not that far apart."

"And then I guess you would certainly say it is not as much as 5/32 of an inch apart; is that right?"

"I am quite sure it is not 5/32."

Haskell read from Dr. McReynolds' deposition of August 14, 1973, in which he stated that the normal distance of separation between sutures was "about an eighth of an inch." He had been asked if the distance could have been 5/32.

"That's a bit much. I don't think I put it more than an eighth of an inch apart."

"4/32 apart. And you could really determine with your eye whether you put it 4/32 or 5/32?"

"Believe me, Counsel, I didn't put a ruler down to look."

"Of course not. . . . Can you swear it was not 5/32?"

"No. I would not swear to anything in that particular category because it is not capable of being proved either way."

21.

"I brought in five expert witnesses . . . but the jurors placed more credence in Dr. Pitts than in all of my experts. He testified impressively, exhibited a basic honesty and integrity, and was willing to concede gray areas. I understand he has been severely criticized by his fellow specialists, but he ought not to be if he testified in accordance with his professional convictions."

—Harold Hunter

Dr. Frederick W. Pitts looked like everyone's notion of the ideal doctor—tall and spare, graying, serious of mien, well-dressed and distinguished-looking. His credentials were almost unbelievably impressive. And although he was testifying for the plaintiff in this case, he had testified for the defense in others, evidently deciding each case on its merits. Harold Hunter's admiration for him was manifest. "Before you came to testify here," he said in his cross-examination, "your name and your very fine reputation were known to me, Doctor."

"Harold Hunter made a serious mistake in telling Dr. Pitts on the stand that his fine reputation had preceded him."
—Haskell Shapiro

Dr. Pitts testified that he often spent as long as eight to ten hours on a severe operation of the type Dr. Spindle had performed on Betty.

"Actually," he said, "the longest I have spent on dissecting one of these things was I believe close to fourteen hours, because you basically take each and every little nerve root. . . . You have to pick up each one of these little fibers and strip it clear, and you have to take special coagulating instruments and you have to burn the tiny blood vessels, coagulate them, that are in the way, and you have to cut them with microsurgical instruments, and so it takes a long time."

According to Dr. Spindle's report, there had been severe scarring about the nerve roots, with actual bone growing through them, with marked calcification and with spicules through the whole lower lumbar area. What did that indicate to Dr. Pitts?

"He describes an advanced significant type of arachnoiditis. . . . It is very unrewarding surgery because the nerve roots are so encased that it is very difficult to get them out without causing even more scar tissue than is there already. . . . You just have to be very meticulous about it. It takes hours and hours."

But Dr. Pitts refused to be pinned down on the issue of how long such an operation ought to take, or takes on the average. There was no such thing as an average, he insisted. It depended on the extent of the arachnoiditis and the technique of the surgeon.

Dr. Spindle's operation had taken two hours and thirty-five minutes. What did that suggest to Dr. Pitts?

"I have never seen Dr. Spindle operate. All I can say is that it is a relatively short period of time for this type of surgery. I don't know if he is an exceptionally fast surgeon or not."

"Dr. Pitts seemed to be the most straightforward and honest of all the witnesses. It was more his mannerisms than anything particular he said. He seemed sure of himself, and above all seemed to be answering the questions according to how he felt, rather than how he thought they should be answered. Many of the other doctors and witnesses, when someone asked them a question, they'd think, 'What's he driving at?' and try to come up with the right answer. But he seemed very open, like he was perfectly willing to answer questions for or against the person he was appearing for. He just laid it on the line the way it was."

—Pete Crosetto

"What Spindle did, these operations, definitely contributed to the insult on her back. But as I am able to judge, in view of the fact that the lady was in pain, had a condition that was not getting better, wanted something done about it, went to a doctor who recommended him, that he should definitely have done what he was able to do for her.

"I feel that quite a number of the defense's witnesses said they likewise found Spindle's procedures adequate, they performed the same way. Were it me, I would have to say, You're the doctor, I don't know a thing about it. That was the way he operated, and if you went to him, that was the operation you were getting. He did a Dr. Spindle operation. Whether Betty Burke should have had better knowledge, I don't know. But she went to him and agreed to the operation. If she felt she hadn't been properly informed, then why did she agree to it? And if she did agree and consent, that's what she bargained for."

—Bob Siemann

112

PART THREE

1.

"The plaintiff brought in Dr. Theodore Kurze, the pioneer of the surgical microscope. Dr. Kurze was not a paragon of humility."

—Harold Hunter

Testimony of Dr. Theodore Kurze, November 9, 1973:

Q. Are you commonly known as one of the founders of the microsurgical microscope?

A. I am thought to have been the first pioneer to have used the microscope in the operating room in neurosurgery. As a matter of fact, I am quite sure I was. . . . I believe that the first operation I did under the microscope was in the peripheral nervous system. Then we went into the head and the brain. . . . Then it became apparent to us that it was extremely valuable in protecting the very small blood vessels that are just as vital as the nerves themselves. Then it was used for repair of intercranial aneurysms. . . . The work that I had done and the universities had done became generally accepted.

The microscope affords the surgeon the opportunity to see much better. The tissue that is being worked on is magnified anywhere from four to thirty times . . .

Q. Does the use of the microsurgical microscope in arachnoiditis operations require much more time than an operation without the microsurgical technique?

A. In order to accomplish the surgical dissection it must be done thoroughly and completely, and therefore it does increase the time necessary to complete the operation. On

115

the other hand, it is not possible to do that thorough a job without the microscope. So therefore it does take longer. Because more is done.

"I thought the microsurgical microscope aspect was impressive. We all thought a lot about that, because of the fact that Spindle wore such thick glasses. Here's a man who can't even see normally, and on top of that he doesn't take advantage of all the means available these days to make things more visible. The defense made one good point, though—that it takes longer when you use the microscope, and the patient is open that much longer and exposed to that much more shock."
—Pete Crosetto

"At first I had doubts on that point; but I really think he should have used whatever he was most comfortable with."
—Kathy Spellman, juror
aged 21, student

Testimony of Dr. McReynolds, October 3:
Q. Did you make any inquiry as to Dr. Spindle's certification status at that time?
A. No, it never occurred to me to ask about that.
Q. Had you ascertained at that time that he was not Board-certified, would that have made any difference?
A. No, I am sure it wouldn't. His work was very, very fine. . . . Whether or not a man actually finished his Board examination and then became certified was sometimes a matter of—of pressure of time and pressure of practice. Because examinations are given after a man has been in practice. And if he takes time out to study up and go for his examinations, this often produces quite a hiatus in his practice . . .
Q. Assuming for a moment that Dr. Spindle had twice taken the exam and twice failed to pass it, would that have had any bearing, had you known this, upon your decision to select him?

A. No, I think not, because I am acquainted with the politics of that particular specialty examination.

Testimony of Dr. Kurze, November 9:

Q. Dr. Kurze, being a member of the American Board of Neurological Surgery, I assume you are familiar with the examination that the Board gives?

A. Yes. I give it.

Q. You give it.

A. And design it.

Q. Oh. You design it. Is that exam given nationwide?

A. Yes.

Q. So it is the same standard nationally?

A. Yes.

Q. Do you believe that the results of passing this, certifying a neurosurgeon or failing him, is that based on political considerations?

A. In no sense of the word whatsoever. We go to extreme lengths to make that impossible. I say that with feeling.

Testimony of Dr. Spindle, October 3:

Q. In performing this surgery, what kind of optical aid did you have?

A. I used an operating loop on my glasses. They come above my glasses and they flip down and they come right over so I can get magnification. About two and a half times.

Q. Is that adequate?

A. For this I felt it was adequate, yes.

Testimony of Dr. Pitts, October 12:

Q. You are not professionally critical of the fact that Dr. Spindle in this case used a surgical loop as an optical aid, are you?

A. I am certainly not critical of his using the loop. I think that the loop was a step in the right direction. I think that he would have been better equipped surgically had he

117

utilized more elaborate microdissection techniques.

Q. Do you feel that failure to use them was a violation of the standard of care?

A. It is hard to know at that time. At this time I think it would be a violation, since the scope is widely available and there have been many courses making it available to people. I think that he probably would have benefited his patient had he used the scope . . .

Q. If I tell you that there is a certain neurosurgeon who failed his exam once, will that bother you a little bit about him?

A. Not too much. A lot of people fail it one time.

Q. Good. If I tell you that this neurosurgeon failed twice, will that now begin to bother you?

A. It would begin to bother me.

"Since they let him be the head of the hospital he must have been qualified."

—Kathy Spellman

2.

Testimony of Dr. Spindle, October 3:

Q. Following one of your operations, the excised tissue which was taken to pathology disclosed among the adhesive material what appeared to be a strand of pinkish gray neuro material?

A. Yes.

Q. Characterized as granular and degenerated?

A. Yes.

Q. Prior to your arrival in court this condition has been characterized more than once as a cut nerve. Did you cut any nerves, sir?

A. I cut no functioning neural tissue. I removed this strand where I could get no demonstrable function and sent it to the pathologist rather than throwing it in the garbage. I wanted to see what it was.

Q. With respect to your last surgery, were there instances where you could not dissect nerve strands from the adhesive material?

A. Oh, yes. It was totally impossible to get some of the nerve strands that were already dead, were growing right through—they had been squeezed to death by the bone.

. . . . .

Q. So with respect to any nerve tissue that went to the pathologist, you predetermined that that was dead nerve in any event?

A. That was my feeling, yes.

Q. Were there any signs or symptoms following either of your operations which even remotely suggested to you that you had cut, injured or sacrificed living viable nerve?

A. No. On the contrary, I felt that I had obviously taken diseased nerve, which was not functioning well, and returned it back to a functioning status.

What color are nerves? It depends on which doctor you ask.

Testimony of Dr. Spindle, October 3:

Q. Doctor, what is the color of functioning neural tissue?

A. Okay. When you are in a diseased state, the coloring, that's very difficult to say. They are not the normal grayish color with grayish white, with some blood vessels. When there is scar tissue among them they haven't had a good blood supply and they may look a denser white. They may be somewhat pinkish.

Q. The color of dead nerve would be what?

A. Well, if you had completely dead nerve it could be dense white like scar. And it could also have pinkish elements from the blood that would be around it in blood vessels.

119

Testimony of Dr. McReynolds, October 2:

Q. Is there any significance, Doctor, to the fact that the color of the nerves was pinkish gray?

A. No.

Q. What is the color of healthy nerves?

A. Oh, almost white, slightly yellowish color.

Q. And the color of dead nerves?

A. Not very much difference.

Testimony of Dr. Van Houten, September 28:

Q. Is it often difficult to dissect dead nerve tissue from adhesive tissue?

A. Yes. But pinkish tissue isn't dead, it is usually living.

Q. Well—

A. The report said, "pinkish gray."

Q. What is the meaning of gray, Doctor?

A. The normal tissue color is gray. But pinkish could indicate some vascularity to it . . .

Q. What color is our skin when it dies?

A. When it dies?

Q. Yes.

A. Gray.

Q. What color is a nerve when it is in the process of dying?

A. Gray.

. . . . .

Q. Sir, the pathologist's report from Downey Hospital that was shown to you by counsel indicated those nerve roots pinkish gray.

A. Correct.

Q. Does that indicate that these nerves were dead?

A. No.

Q. Therefore some of these nerves, would you conclude, would you not, that they were alive?

A. Right.

Why does a surgeon write an operating report? Again, it depends on which surgeon you ask.

Testimony of Dr. Pitts, October 12:

Q. What is the purpose when a surgeon writes the operative notes, could you tell us?

A. Well, it is basically to provide a record of what he did find and what he did do, so that at a later date he can refer to it, if the case should arise, or to allow other surgeons who may have to deal with a subsequent problem of the patient to be informed as to what went on . . .

Testimony of Dr. McReynolds:

Q. Is one of the reasons for having good records to be able to have them in case you are not available for further care, and another doctor has to take over?

A. No, this is a habit that doctors develop. They either have a habit of making records, or they have a habit of not making informative records. And this seems to be a characteristic of the man rather than any situation that threatens him or is a demand on him.

3.

On November 21, 1969, after he had operated on Betty, Dr. Spindle wrote to Dr. Albert Cole, a radiologist, asking him to examine Betty Burke and determine whether radiation treatment would be beneficial to her. He wrote, "I have felt that post-operative radiation in these patients tends to prevent recurrence."

In December of the same year, he sent to Haskell Shapiro's office copies of his operating reports on Betty. In the accompanying letter, he wrote, "It is a bit of a question whether radiation is beneficial in such cases as hers to prevent recurrence. Some feel it is and some feel it perhaps may even cause more problems; however, I have seen some good results from radiation to prevent recurrences."

Betty did receive radiation treatment. It did not appear to benefit her.

Questioning Dr. Spindle on the witness stand, David Sabih asked why he had suggested radiation therapy. Naturally, because he thought it would help, Dr. Spindle replied. What was his authority for this opinion? Dr. Spindle named Dr. Arthur Silverman, a well-known radiologist, as one of the authorities in the field who believed in and recommended radiation in cases such as Betty's.

David Sabih contacted Dr. Silverman, who said that he did not treat arachnoiditis with radiation. Had he ever told Dr. Spindle that? "Of course." David asked Dr. Silverman to testify; he refused, was subpoenaed, and finally agreed to testify as an expert witness.

On the stand, Dr. Silverman was again asked if he had told Dr. Spindle that he never treated arachnoiditis with radiation. He said he did not remember. He did not believe arachnoiditis should get radiation treatment, but he did not remember telling that to Dr. Spindle.

Testimony of Dr. McReynolds:
"The first recorded effort to control arachnoiditis was the use of radiation back in 1926. I think it was also tried along in the 1940's. No one was impressed with it enough so that it was established as an effective control. . . . It really hasn't been demonstrated to show, to produce any real benefit."

4.

A few weeks into the trial, Betty Burke called Haskell Shapiro. She had been thinking about the possibility that she might win her case, and it had occurred to her that if she received any money, her husband would want some of it. During one of their periods of separation—1964, it was—Gene had filed for a divorce, but so far as she knew it had never been granted, and then they had gotten together again.

Haskell sent for the records of the divorce suit. Gene Burke had filed for divorce on the grounds of "extreme cruelty." In the traditional legal language, his wife had "caused him to suffer and endure extreme mental and physical pain and suffering, all of which has destroyed his peace of mind and happiness, impaired his health, completely destroyed and defeated the legitimate objects of matrimony, and made it utterly impossible for him to live with defendant as her husband."

A final decree had been issued on September 29, 1965: Betty and Gene Burke were divorced. He would have no claims on her.

5.

"I think lawyers are businessmen, and if they see an opportunity for a case, they're going to take it, particularly if they stand a chance of getting some money. That's what they're in business for. I don't know that they chase ambulances and that sort of thing, maybe some do; but I don't think these particular lawyers were less than honest. I've never had any dealings with lawyers, but I hear a lot about them, that they're dishonest. But I can't hardly swallow that a profession that old and that necessary for our way of life can be all bad. Lawyers are professional people, and I feel would be honest as much as they can, though they're not above stretching the truth a little to further their cause."

—Bob Siemann

"By far, Mr. Hunter was the most impressive of the three lawyers. He gave the impression of being the polished, self-assured professional that most people would think of lawyers as being. It appeared he knew every question he was going to ask. He was rarely surprised.

"The team of Shapiro and Sabih—at the time my impres-

123

sion was that Sabih was the young, eager, new lawyer, anxious to do everything, and Shapiro was the stabilizer, who let him go as far as he knew he could go without fouling up, gave him so much rein, and at the right moment would yank on him and keep things in control. Most of the jury felt that Shapiro was very accomplished, extremely intelligent, knew just what to do at the right time. But he wasn't an orator, he was very, very soft-spoken. But it was a good combination, because we could take just so much of Sabih, his motions and overbearing attitude, and then all of a sudden you'd have a nice, quiet, relaxing period.

"I thought that Hunter at all times knew more what he was doing. But just because of that, Sabih and Shapiro did a much more thorough job. Certainly in the course of the trial they turned over a lot of stones that didn't need turning over, but they didn't miss any either."

—Pete Crosetto

"Mr. Hunter was really an eloquent speaker. He had a beautiful way with words. Mr. Sabih was very dramatic, and for what he was doing drama was important. But Mr. Shapiro's quietness was as important as Sabih's drama."

—Kathy Spellman

"Mr. Sabih is very energetic and active—he struck me as immature, like a big kid. I got tired of listening to him hammer away at the same thing. As for Shapiro, he was just the opposite; I don't know how to say it, it almost seemed like he wasn't interested. I don't think I would really care to have either of them handle a case for me."

—Bob Siemann

"The tenacity of plaintiff's counsel, especially Mr. Sabih, vastly outweighed his obvious inexperience—it was translated to the jury in terms of real honest-to-God sincerity. He wouldn't easily surrender a point. But he was never less than a gentleman. The hours and efforts of this young man showed through. He was one of the plaintiff's most formidable weapons."

—Harold Hunter

6.

"There were some inconsistencies in Mrs. Burke's testimony. I tried to delicately and politely impeach her, to discredit her testimony as gently and tastefully as I could."

—Harold Hunter

"She seemed not to be asking for sympathy. She seemed very strong, as though she were telling us that she'd work it out."

—Verla Holloway

"I was afraid to look at Betty, afraid of too much sympathy."

—Emma Oaks

"She's been made to suffer, and she deserved to try to get everything she could."

—Dolores Loya

Betty Burke testified on October 16. She was wheeled to the stand on a gurney, a sort of bed on wheels. David Sabih questioned her.

Q. Are you comfortable, Betty?

A. Yes. Yes, sir.

Q. All right. Okay. Are you in a gurney pursuant to any instructions?

A. I am. The doctor wrote orders that it's the only way I could come, because I now have some decubiti on my—I can't sit up for very long at a time, and that's the only reason I am on the gurney.

. . . . .

Q. Could you tell His Honor and the jury, how does your condition now affect your life?

A. Well, in many ways. I can't do any of the things I used to do. I can't do anything with my family. I can't go places. I'm very restricted in what I can do. Before I go to see anybody, I have to make sure if they have steps; if they do, if there is a man there that can get me up them. And if there are too many steps, I can't go. Many, many things.

I can go to a drive-in movie if I lay down in the back of the station wagon. It's just—anywhere you go has to be planned according to how many steps you have, who is there to take you. And then the tolerance time that I can sit up pretty well limits what I can do.

Betty said that Dr. Spindle had given her laxatives when she had lost control over her bowels and was removing fecal matter by hand.

"I quit taking the laxatives because then I just went everywhere. I mean, I could be anywhere, in bed with my husband or in transit on the wheelchair or—I never knew. I would just go everywhere."

"Did you in fact soil the bed?"

"Often."

"With your husband?"

"Yes. And I preferred doing it the other way than—I mean, let's face it, nobody wants to—you know—"

. . . . .

Q. Was there any urinary problem—what is that exactly, what is the problem there?

A. Well, I had a Foley for quite a while. A Foley is a tube in you that goes into a bag. You carry it or you have one that goes on your leg. And you are sitting somewhere and pretty soon it is full. And then my family doctor put me in the hospital, because I kept having very bad infections and they backed up into my kidneys. And a urologist, that kind of doctor, cut the hole where I urinate and made it bigger and took out the Foley. And that's when I learned to press my stomach and force my bladder.

Q. In other words, you can't use your bladder naturally, you have to always press on it to urinate?

A. Yes.

I have a spinal column stimulator. It is an experimental thing. It's an electric thing. You put it on each side of your back and it controls—you can control the width of it. And it don't shock you like you think electricity will, but it will make the pain go away without taking medicine. But so far it only works laying down.

Harold Hunter cross-examined Betty:

Q. Did Dr. McReynolds tell you how the cyst was caused?

A. He said it was like an abscess; that it was relatively common with surgeries, not necessarily just back surgeries, any surgery.

Q. Nothing was said about a leak of spinal fluid?

A. There was nothing said to me about spinal fluid ever. Not until 1971.

Q. When you heard testimony at the auto accident trial about spinal fluid?

A. Yes.

Hunter read a portion of Betty's testimony from that trial:

"Q. Were you ever informed that you had a leak of spinal fluid?

"A. Oh, yes."

Q. Mrs. Burke, no one appreciates better than I that this was a good two years ago when this testimony was given.

A. Uh-huh.

Q. Do you have anything that you would like to add to it? In other words, it appears to me that at the trial of the auto case you testified under oath that you were aware of the leakage.

MR. SABIH: Your Honor, I object.

THE WITNESS: Not of leakage of spinal fluid.

MR. HUNTER: Well—

THE COURT: You were going to object?

MR. SABIH: I object. I think counsel is misleading. They are talking about these operations conducted by Dr. Spindle.

MR. HUNTER: I don't mean to mislead the witness. I will withdraw the question. Mrs. Burke, you were asked specifically, "Were you ever informed that you had a leak of the fluid?" And you stated, "Oh, yes."

A. Well, yes. The fluid was leaking out on my bed all the time. I was never told it was spinal fluid.

Q. But you were told that the leakage was coming from the caudal sac?

A. I assumed that was this walnut sac he stuck the needle in, on my back. That the abscess was in.

But the most damaging inconsistency in Betty's testimony, between the present and the earlier trial, concerned her physical condition before the August, 1969 auto accident. Harold Hunter cross-examined:

Q. You recognized at that time that if you were to recover any damages from Mr. Kuykendall it was of utmost importance that the cause of your injuries be proved to be attributable to the automobile accident.

A. The doctors had told me that—that the condition I was in was because of the car accident.

Q. And you knew at the time that case was in trial that it was important to establish that the accident caused all of your physical problems?

A. I believed it.

128

Q. You believed it in spite of the back pain that was existing up to and including the day of the accident?
A. Yes.

Clearly skeptical, Harold Hunter read from the transcript of the auto accident trial:

"Q. Mrs. Burke, prior to the August of 1969, the date of the automobile accident, had you been planning to have another operation?
"A. I wasn't even planning to see a doctor. I was as healthy as you are . . .
"Q. Did you have any symptoms whatsoever in the months immediately preceding this accident?
"A. No, I didn't.
"Q. For about how long had you been symptom-free?
"A. I would say, eight, nine months or more.
"Q. You were feeling good?
"A. I mean absolutely symptom-free, just nothing wrong.
"Q. Prior to the accident of 1969, you were back to all of your normal activities?
"A. Yes.
"Q. No exceptions?
"A. Even water surfing.
"Q. Beg your pardon?
"A. Even surfing.
"Q. You yourself were surfing?
"A. Yes. I had been surfing two days before the accident."

Yet when Betty was questioned by her own attorneys—and in her deposition as well—she had spoken of physical problems during those months preceding the accident, problems she had been told she would have to "learn to live with":
"I would lay down so long and then be up so long. The

right leg, I had weakness. I had to cater to it because it was painful."

Obviously, she could not have been "absolutely symptom-free," as she had testified at the auto accident trial, if she had had these physical problems. In fact, she had lost that earlier case precisely because the jury had found it impossible to believe that the accident had caused all her problems.

Harold Hunter's questioning succeeded in convincing some of the present jury that, while Betty might not deliberately have lied at the first trial in the hope of collecting damages, she had stretched the truth a little; and because of that, she forfeited a little of their sympathy.

7.

Betty's first myelogram, in March, 1967, had been done by Drs. Evans and Peterson. Dr. Peterson, who had taken the pictures, had written in his radiological report that nine cc. of Pantopaque had been utilized. His report said nothing about the removal of the dye; but Dr. Peterson testified on October 17 that the dye was always removed after the pictures were taken. A few droplets always remained, he said—less than one cc.

He testified that he had not noted the removal of the dye in his report because there was no reason to do so: it was understood that it was always removed.

But Dr. McReynolds had testified that during surgery he had removed two to three cc. of Pantopaque, a fairly significant quantity; and that the slit in the dura which later leaked spinal fluid and caused a cyst to form had been made for that commendable purpose—to remove excess dye that the radiologists had left in.

"The final films," Dr. McReynolds had said, "showed a large amount of Pantopaque still remaining." In addition, Betty had complained before her surgery of a full feeling in the tail-bone, and this frequently indicated a large residue of Pantopaque in the spinal canal. "Large amounts of Pantopaque are not desirable," said Dr. McReynolds.

Both men could not be correct. Someone was either mistaken or being less than candid.

"I assume McReynolds was honest, and if he said he found dye, he found dye. I don't assume the other man was lying, I feel he was mistaken. Somehow this time he failed to remove it all."

—Bob Siemann

"I didn't actually feel any of them were deliberately lying, but we all want to make ourselves look as good as possible."

—Verla Holloway

Haskell Shapiro, in his concluding argument on November 13, said, "You will recall that Dr. McReynolds testified that he saw the last film or films that showed that there was still some Pantopaque left. But when he was cross-examined about that he readily admitted that he had done 300 myelograms and never took out Pantopaque and then took another film. He never heard of any radiologist who did that, and he didn't have any explanation as to why it would have been done in this case."

The fact that he saw Pantopaque in the last film, then, would have been no indication that it was not removed.

8.

When David Sabih was looking for expert witnesses to testify, the Bar Association had given him the name of a Dr. Virgil Partridge as someone who was completely unbiased. David and Haskell went to see Dr. Partridge and paid him $100 for his time. He said that in his opinion it would be wrong to use Surgicel to stop a dural leak; he had known of

131

patients who died as a result of the use of Surgicel.

But when he was asked to testify for the plaintiff, Dr. Partridge refused. Instead, he testified for the defense, and said on the witness stand that the use of Surgicel was acceptable.

Dr. McReynolds had said that he assumed there was Pantopaque remaining in Betty's spine because he had seen it in the last film. Dr. Partridge was asked whether myelogram films are taken after the Pantopaque is removed. Naming two radiologists as his authorities, he said that they were. Haskell Shapiro checked the addresses of these two radiologists: their addresses were the same as that of Dr. Partridge.

Later in his testimony, after the lunch break, Dr. Partridge volunteered the information that he had spoken to those two radiologists during the break, and they had corrected him: they did not take pictures after the dye was removed.

He was asked how long it would have taken to sew up the dural defect instead of using Surgicel. Dr. McReynolds himself had testified that it was "no big thing," it would have taken him only five or ten minutes. Certainly he had not used the Surgicel in order to save himself some time.

Dr. Partridge was not aware of Dr. McReynolds' testimony. "Counsel, it is not that simple a thing," he said. "It would take you between forty and forty-five minutes. This is not that easy an operation."

Could the slit in the dura have been made accidentally? It was possible, said Dr. Partridge. The instruments used in a laminectomy sometimes accidentally cut the dura. "Misadventures" did happen.

Haskell Shapiro asked Dr. Partridge how big the hole in the dura would have to be to require suturing. The size of the hole is not the crucial factor, he replied. If the hole is leaking spinal fluid at the completion of the operation, it should be sewn, regardless of its size.

Dr. Partridge did not know Dr. McReynolds had testified that spinal fluid was still leaking when the operation was over.

The defense may have regretted that Dr. Partridge had agreed to testify for them.

9.

"Every human being of adult years and of sound mind has a right to determine what shall be done with his own body, and a surgeon who performs an operation without his patient's consent commits an assault, for which he is liable in damages."

This famous statement by Justice Benjamin Cardozo in 1914 clarified the applicability of one of the fundamental concepts of Anglo-American law—the right of self-determination —to the field of medicine and surgery, where it has come to be known as the doctrine of informed consent. Inherent in this doctrine is the individual's right to know all the risks involved in a contemplated medical procedure and to refuse to submit to any procedure even though his physicians may consider such a refusal unwise.

Few principles of law have caused more controversy than that of informed consent. Three recent decisions *(Cobbs v. Grant, Canterbury v. Spence,* and *Wilkenson v. Vesey),* which clarified further the legal ramifications of the doctrine in medical malpractice cases, brought an avalanche of protest from the medical profession against what it saw as an infringement upon its rights and an unfair burden of responsibility.

Actually, it has long been recognized in law that the rules of conduct in a fiduciary relationship (one based upon trust) must be different from the "let the buyer beware" ethics of ordinary business relationships. In situations in which a professional—doctor, lawyer, teacher, architect—possesses a far greater degree of knowledge than his client, the professional is obligated to give the client enough information to enable the client to make an intelligent decision. If any harm results from the professional's failure to do so, he makes himself liable to a charge of either battery or negligence.

The *Canterbury v. Spence* decision stated: "It is normally impossible to obtain a consent worthy of its name unless the

133

physician first elucidates the options and the perils for the patient's edification." The doctor must make clear all of the patient's choices (whether surgery, conservative treatment, chemotherapy, no treatment at all), and all the hazards attendant upon each of these choices. This requirement, however, may place the doctor in a difficult position: since he must put the welfare of his patient above all other considerations, he may feel that such complete information would alarm the patient and cause him to make an unwise decision.

The courts, recognizing that the patient's mental and emotional condition is an important factor in the practice of medicine, have allowed physicians a certain amount of discretion in providing information—have, in effect, allowed them to use their judgment in reconciling total disclosure with the best interests of the patient. In the case of *Salgo v. Leland Stanford Jr. University Board of Trustees,* the court said that "each patient presents a separate problem . . . in discussing the element of risk a certain amount of discretion must be employed consistent with the full disclosure of facts necessary to an informed consent." The problem lies in determining how far that "certain amount of discretion" may go in limiting disclosure.

Courts have recognized some situations in which the limiting of disclosure may be justified: an emergency, in which death or serious damage will probably occur if treatment is not given immediately; cases in which a patient clearly cannot cope with disclosure; cases in which the patient requests that he not be fully informed. But a doctor who withholds information because of a patient's mental state would do well to remember that he may later have the burden of proving that mental state; and if he limits disclosure at his patient's request, he had better have the patient put the request in writing and sign it.

There are other situations in which total disclosure may not be required. For instance, the court in *Cobbs v. Grant* stated that there is no need to disclose "relatively minor risks inherent in common procedures when it is common knowledge that such risks inherent in the procedure are of very low incidence." The presumption here is that "everyone knows" of these inherent risks. But again, as with the "certain amount of discretion," the wording is vague. Who decides which risks are "common knowledge" and which are not?

Canterbury v. Spence stated that full disclosure means, in practice, disclosure of only those hazards that are "material to the patient's decision." But who is better qualified to judge the materiality of any factor—doctor or patient? Frequently, it is the jury who must decide what should or should not have been disclosed.

Many doctors dislike the implications of these recent court decisions. The *Bulletin of the Los Angeles County Medical Association* published a satirical "surgery consent form" in which the patient attests to his knowledge of possible complications in a hernia operation:

1. Large artery may be cut and I may bleed to death.

2. Large vein may be cut and I may bleed to death.

3. Tube from testicle may be cut. I will then be sterile on that side.

4. Artery or veins to testicles may be cut—same result.

5. Clot may develop in one or both legs which may cripple me, lead to loss of one or both legs, go to my lungs, or make my veins no good for life.

6. I may develop a horrible infection that may kill me.

7. The hernia may come back after it has been operated on.

8. I may die from general anesthesia.

9. I may be paralyzed from spinal anesthesia.

10. If ether is used, it could explode inside me.

11. I may slip in hospital bathroom.

12. The hospital may burn down.

The patient also indicates, in this mock form, that he fully understands "the anatomy of the body, the pathology of the development of hernia, the surgical technique that will be used to repair the hernia, the physiology of wound healing, the dietetic chemistry of the foods that I must eat to cause healing . . ." and so on. The signatures include those of the patient, his lawyer, the doctor's lawyer, the hospital's lawyer, the anesthetist's lawyer, and a notary public.

But despite the medical profession's scorn, informed consent is the law. As the Cobbs decision made clear, "a minicourse in medical science is not required; the patient is concerned with the risk of death or bodily harm, and problems of recuperation."

There are those who argue that the threat of malpractice suits causes doctors to consider their own protection over the welfare of their patients. Others contend that malpractice suits act as disciplinary and corrective measures to the medical profession. But it matters little which point of view is closer to the truth if the end result is that doctors make fuller disclosures to their patients.

"They didn't explain the consequences to her. Dr. McReynolds said he never told the patient anything they didn't have to know. I didn't like his attitude about not being thorough with his patients. He should have told Betty that Spindle wasn't certified. I feel that a patient should be told everything."

—Dolores Loya

Testimony of Dr. McReynolds:

Q. Dr. McReynolds, you stated yesterday that it was not your custom and practice to explain to patients with medical precision what you intend to do. I believe you told us in essence that this was your prerogative and this was one of the reasons the patient entrusted herself or himself to your judgment. You don't mean by that that you don't feel that the patient should know what is going to be undertaken?

A. No. I attempt to explain to the patient and responsible relatives as near as I can, as much as I have reason to think they will understand about the problems of whatever procedure we anticipate.

Q. Do you consider that you have a duty to obtain the patient's okay or consent before you go ahead with something?

136

A. Certainly I do, yes. I frequently say to the patient, "You know, you can always say no. Always say no."

Q. Before you proceeded with the second operation on May 2, 1967, did you get Betty's consent?

A. Yes, I did.

Q. Did you explain in essence what you were going to do?

A. Yes, I am sure she understood what the problem essentially was. . . . How much actual communication between me and Betty got across, as far as getting information to her was concerned, I have no way of knowing really . . .

Q. Did you tell her what caused the cyst?

A. I don't know that I told her what caused the cyst, except that I thought it was a leak of spinal fluid and that we intended to get rid of the cyst by closing the leak.

Q. Did you tell her, Doctor, what caused the leak of the spinal fluid?

A. No. I don't know that I discussed the reason why it was leaking.

Testimony of Betty Burke:

Q. Did any physician ever tell you that there was a good probability that the surgery might not do you any good at all?

A. No, or I wouldn't have let them operate.

. . . . .

Q. When Dr. McReynolds told you that you needed an operation, did he tell you about any alternatives?

A. No. He assured me that it was done, you know, something done very regularly and not to be upset or worried about it.

Q. Did he tell you about any risks or hazards that you may face from the operation?

A. No. He just assured me it was—everything would be all right, that it was a relatively—that they do it, like, really often.

Q. Okay. So he didn't tell you that paralysis may ensue?

A. No. I think if he had of, I would have got up and run out.

Testimony of Dr. Spindle:

Q. What did you tell Betty prior to that second operation that you performed?

A. I had a long talk with her. I described the risk to her. I told her that our chances of success were minuscule and that it usually was a one-shot deal. Usually wouldn't go in again. But she had had another myelogram, and it did indeed show a complete block, and if she was willing and would accept the possibility of failure or worsening of her condition, then I would operate.

Q. What did she say in response?

A. Well, I think she signed the consent and said, "Let's go on."

Testimony of Betty Burke:

Q. Did Dr. Spindle discuss with you whether there were any risks or hazards to the operation?

A. I talked very little with Dr. Spindle. He just asked me had Dr. McReynolds explained everything to me, that I was going to surgery and that he was operating. I said yes. And that Dr. McReynolds had said it was necessary because there was some kind of a block. And that's about the extent of it.

10.

On October 15, Harold Hunter made a tentative offer to settle the case for $200,000. Betty Burke and her attorneys turned it down.

On October 18, Haskell Shapiro wrote to Harold Hunter:

"On behalf of my client Betty Burke, I am hereby offering to settle all her claims against your clients for the total sum of $475,000, a figure well below the combined insurance limits of the policies of Drs. McReynolds and Spindle; in fact, below the limit of either one alone. This offer is not negotiable. I will hold this offer of settlement open until Tuesday, October 23, 1973 at 9:45 A.M.

"I sincerely believe that considering the present posture of this case, we will be successful if the case goes to a jury verdict, and the jury award will be far in excess of Dr. McReynolds' policy limit, thereby subjecting him to a risk of personal liability in addition to his liability covered by insurance.

"I sincerely believe that we will convince the jury that Dr. McReynolds' testimony that he purposely made a needle puncture is unbelievable. You are aware of all the evidence. Therefore, I feel that if this case is not settled, Dr. McReynolds is being subjected to the risk of a substantial judgment against him for punitive damages."

By October 23 at 9:45 A.M., the offer had not been accepted.

"I had no way of knowing how the case would turn out. That letter was just part of the negotiations. Just wishful thinking."

—Haskell Shapiro

11.

In his deposition, Dr. McReynolds had attributed Betty's paralysis in large part to an allergic reaction to the Pantopaque dye used in her first myelogram of March, 1967. Nevertheless, in August, 1969, after her automobile accident, he had taken another myelogram. Before Betty's last operation of December, 1970, a third myelogram had been done.

Testimony of Dr. McReynolds:

Q. Now, Doctor, there has been much testimony about your belief that Pantopaque might be one of the factors leading to arachnoiditis. Did you have that belief prior to August 22, 1969, when Betty Burke was given her second myelogram?

A. Oh, yes, I did.

Q. All right. In spite of this belief, Doctor, did you feel that Pantopaque could nonetheless be introduced at that time without further effect?

A. Oh, yes. She still had Pantopaque in her canal. Putting more in wouldn't change the situation basically . . .

Q. And did you feel that the necessity of proper investigation outweighed any risk there may have been of introducing additional Pantopaque?

A. Oh, yes, I certainly felt that.

Q. Your opinion now is that she is allergic to the dye, is it not?

A. No, I think not in the sense that you imply. Her local tissue reaction to the Pantopaque dye, from the original injection, was an unusual abnormal reaction response to the presence of Pantopaque plus the other factors of trauma of surgery and ruptured disk . . . it is a localized over-response to the presence of the dye.

Q. Isn't that an allergy?

A. Well, it is a similar type of response that you refer to vaguely as an allergy. This is not an exact term that you are using. There are no exact terms that I know of to use.

In his deposition, however, Dr. McReynolds had been asked whether a reaction such as Betty's would be "a situation where the patient is allergic to the dye."

"I have assumed that this is true," he had answered.

"The doctors've got you over a barrel, they can double-talk all afternoon, and who knows what they're talking about?"
—Pete Crosetto

Closing argument by Mr. Shapiro, November 13, 1973:

"You will all recall that Dr. McReynolds testified at one time that in his opinion it was the Pantopaque dye that caused her arachnoiditis. . . . It wasn't the surgeries, it wasn't anything else, it was that only—the Pantopaque dye.

"A little later on, he tells us on the witness stand, I think I went too hard on the Pantopaque. When he was asked why he changed his mind, he didn't know . . .

"Why did he no longer think so? Because at this time he realized that if it were true that he thought that Pantopaque was the incriminating factor, he knew that as a good doctor he should not have used Pantopaque again in 1969 and once again in 1970. It was an untenable position . . .

"I would much rather believe that he never believed at all, at any time, that Pantopaque was the culprit. I would much rather believe that, than to think that even though he believed it, he was willing to take that risk with Betty Burke again in '69 and again in '70, and then tell us lamely that, Well, she already had arachnoiditis so the Pantopaque wouldn't hurt her . . .

"I just can't believe that as a conscientious doctor he ever believed that the Pantopaque was what caused it."

12.

The medical testimony went on and on. Doctor after eminent doctor took the stand, recited his qualifications—where he had gone to school, which hospitals he had practiced in, what articles he had written—and, under cross-examination by the opposing side, each reluctantly told where his operating privileges had been curtailed and what malpractice charges had been filed against him. Using charts, diagrams and blackboard, the doctors explained the structure of the spine and of the dural canal; the nature, symptoms, possible causes and treatment of the mysterious and apparently incurable condition, with which the jurors had become all too familiar, known as arachnoiditis. Juror Pete Crosetto, the law student, who spent his evenings studying for the bar exam, began having great difficulty staying awake, and was nearly admonished by the judge, who kept looking at him disapprovingly.

The defense began to present its witnesses on October 18. Dr. Spindle took the stand again. He testified that he had never refused treatment because a patient could not pay. He stressed that he had never discussed fees with Betty, and had *never* turned a patient over to a collection agency.

Testimony of Betty Burke: "He asked me how I was going to pay for it."

A Mr. Kane, who handled Dr. Spindle's accounts, testified that while it was true Dr. Spindle had never refused to treat a patient for financial reasons, he had turned over some of his accounts to collection agencies. Mr. Kane believed Betty's account had been one of them.

Dr. Spindle testified that when he opened the dura during his first operation on Betty, he found "a mess." The nerve roots resembled "a ball of string with honey on it." She had had vaginal numbness and bowel problems before he ever saw her.

Testimony of Betty Burke:
Q. Betty, before the third operation, did you have any problems with bowel control or urinary bladder problems?
A. Somewhat, bowel control, yes.
Q. Was there numbness in the vagina?
A. No, not at that time.
Q. That numbness developed after the third operation?
A. Yes.

Before his second operation on Betty, Dr. Spindle said, he had carefully explained to her that there was not much chance of success. He had even mentioned that people sometimes died in surgery. She had urged him to operate no matter how small the chance that it would help her.

Testimony of Betty Burke:

Q. Prior to the fourth surgery, did Dr. Spindle tell you whether there were any risks or hazards associated with that surgery?

A. Dr. Spindle said very little to me again. He just asked me the same question again, how was I going to pay for it. I told him this time I had insurance.

Some of the statements Dr. Spindle had made at the auto accident trial were read to him by the plaintiff's attorneys. "I'm much impressed," he said, "that I made basically the same statements then as I have now. You scared me; I thought you were going to trip me up or something."

The defense called Anne Gridjan, a registered nurse. She testified that paraplegics normally can do everyday tasks like driving and shopping; that they tend to make more friends than they had had before; that only one out of 750 to 1000 paraplegics she had seen needed constant nursing; that 25% to 35% of paraplegics and quadriplegics were working.

Under cross-examination, she explained that by "working," she had meant either working or in training. Actually, only 10% of paraplegics and quadriplegics were gainfully employed at any given time. She went on to say that 75% of paraplegics were bowel-trained. They might have an occasional accident. The other 25% were not well trained and might be expected to have more frequent accidents.

There was a tendency to suicide among paraplegics.

In his re-direct examination, Harold Hunter elicited the information that the primary cause of death among paraplegics was respiratory disease. Suicide held only second place.

The defense called as one of its expert witnesses Dr. William McColl, a former professional football player. He was a big, husky man, red-haired, full of nervous energy. David Sabih asked him the approximate distance between the dura and the arachnoid. He replied that he didn't think that was important. He just stuck the needle in till fluid came out. It was like throwing a football—the distance didn't matter, the important thing was whether you caught it or not.

Was the angle of the needle important? Yes, that was important, Dr. McColl said. Just as with a bullet entering the body, the angle was important because it affected the distance.

"Let us assume, just for a moment," David Sabih said, "that Dr. McReynolds did not put the needle in with the force of a bullet." The jurors laughed; the spectators laughed; even the judge permitted himself the briefest of smiles. For a moment, the tension was broken and the grim proceedings lightened.

"When defense started bringing their witnesses, I practically swung over to plaintiff's side. I didn't like some of the witnesses defense produced, they looked like a bunch of—one guy in particular, acted like a clown and he was supposed to be a neurosurgeon—big fellow, played football at one time or another, red hair, jumped around a lot. I thought defense produced a far stronger case with cross-examination of plaintiff's witnesses than with their own. Some of 'em struck me as just not the kind I would consider competent, whereas plaintiff presented some very high-ranking doctors."

—Bob Siemann

"At the end of the plaintiff's case I was almost leaning toward a verdict for the defense—until Hunter brought on his witnesses. They were so obviously pro-doctor and there to protect their profession, that Hunter ruined his case."

—Pete Crosetto

"The defense was very strong in the multitude and forcefulness of our expert witnesses."

—Harold Hunter

A neurosurgeon, Dr. Dean Hope, testified that the decision as to when surgery was necessary was strictly a matter of the surgeon's judgment. Dr. McReynolds had acted properly in operating when he did.

The decision not to suture the dura had also been perfectly proper. Often, slits an inch long were left in the dura, sometimes with the arachnoid bulging through—and there were no ill effects.

Dr. Hope felt that Betty Burke probably would have been totally paralyzed within six to twelve months after the third operation, even if the fourth had never been done.

The defense called one more expert witness, Dr. John McRae. Everything that Dr. McReynolds had done, he stated, was within the standard of care.

"The doctors, they'd quibble, they'd say something was within the standard of care but they wouldn't do it themselves . . ."

Verla Holloway

Dr. McReynolds was called to the stand again. He said he had, in his experience, observed patients with spinal fluid leaks that continued for five or six weeks and then spontaneously closed. It was better to wait than to invade an area that had already been operated on. It was a matter of judgment.

Testimony of Dr. McReynolds:

Q. You felt it was a matter of judgment just to put the Surgicel on it?

A. Yes. Both Dr. Mooney and I felt that it was just a matter of judgment.

Testimony of Dr. Van Houten:

A. I don't think that a surgeon should take that risk with his patient, to leave a spinal fluid leak, and leave it open and expect a little piece of Surgicel like this to seal it off.

145

Q. As far as you are concerned, it falls outside the realm of permissible judgment; is that right? . . .

A. I don't believe that is in the realm of judgment, Counsel. I think that's a matter of just good surgery.

Closing argument of Mr. Shapiro, November 13:

"When Dr. Sanford Kornblum was asked, 'Is this a matter of judgment as to whether to sew it or not?' his answer, you might recall, was, 'Well, everything is a matter of judgment, but it is below the standard of care.' That's the critical point.

"Of course it is true everything could be a matter of judgment. If that were the test, then there could never be negligence.

"As a matter of fact, you will probably recall that when Dr. Spindle was on the stand and he was asked, 'What would be the standard of care in this situation?' he told us that so long as the doctor was competent, whatever in his judgment was the right thing to do—which means in effect that a doctor cannot make a mistake . . ."

"When there was a doctor for the plaintiff, I was thinking their way, and when there was one for the defendants, I was thinking their way. I actually did not have any idea, when I went in to deliberate, which way I was going to vote and I really don't think anybody else did, either. We were all mixed up and tired and scared."

—Roseann Halte

"Quite some time before the case was over, about two weeks before the end, I felt quite sure how we were going to go. But some time earlier than that, I made up my mind that was the way I wanted it to go and I was going to try to sway the jury."

—Pete Crosetto

146

13.

David Sabih, in his rather erratic English, made his closing statement on November 12. "I am very nervous," he said, "because there is so much at stake and I am praying that God will help me in letting what the thoughts are in my mind come out to you. Still I am going to be very fair and give you the evidence exactly as it developed. . . . I mention to you the following facts that are sort of circumstantial, but when you add it up together the jigsaw puzzle will not become a puzzle, it will indicate what the facts are really true."

He spoke all day, in his uncertain but colorful English—gesturing excitedly, bouncing around, taking the fullest possible advantage of the drama and pathos in his client's history. He entertained his audience with a one-man show.

In his conclusion he compared Betty Burke's situation with that of a child buried by his playmates in the sand: "They run away, not to help him out, and the boy tries to get out. He can't get out. So all the sand is all over him and he can't get out and he worries and he looks and there is sometimes the waves that are coming in and he is worried whether the waves are going to come near him. You can look at that boy's face and he doesn't want to show you he is crying, but eventually there is so much anxiety, so much worry that you will see the tears. He says, Get me out, get me out.

"This is what Betty is telling you . . . But no playmates will come to get Betty out of the crippled body and give her back the healthy one."

David Sabih asked the jury to give Betty the next best thing: the chance to live without being dependent.

"I knew everyone was trying to read our faces. So I was determined to put on a card player's face, no expression."
—Roseann Halte

"The most nerve-wracking thing in the world is trying to read a jury."

"I laid out an approach that I thought was equitable to everybody. We took each of what I considered the salient points—there were eighteen of them. We'd go over each one and consider the four elements, that is, duty, breach, causation and damage—the elements necessary for a negligence case—and decide whether or not we could find all four on any of the salient points. It turned out to be a very lengthy process. . . .

"I thought there was a strong inference that the slit in the dura was an accident, that McReynolds had slipped. He looked at it and thought, Oops. But it wouldn't be any big thing, he wouldn't purposely close the woman up if he thought there were going to be complications. There's a fine distinction between negligence and poor judgment. Lord knows any doctor can be wrong, any time it involves judgment. He chose not to close up the slit. He was wrong, but not negligent. It was when he called Spindle in to botch up an already bad mistake that the negligence came in. McReynolds was very aware of Spindle's reputation and the fact that he could not pass the neurosurgeons' certifying examination. It was brought out very clearly in the trial that Spindle left a lot to be desired as far as a neurosurgeon goes. It appeared that McReynolds brought Spindle in because he thought he'd do a quick job and not say anything about what happened."

—Pete Crosetto

"As far as I was concerned, the whole thing was the slit in the dura. That was the big mistake."

—Emma Oaks

"It could have been an accidental cut. But the fact that he tried to cover up was wrong."

—Dolores Loya

The trial had lasted nine weeks. The jury's deliberations took nine days.

While the jury was out, Harold Hunter made an offer of $250,000. It was refused.

"I'm sure that in my heart I never doubted, never wavered, or I would never have said no to $250,000."

"There were no heated discussions in the jury room, although we certainly didn't agree, and we discussed the points quite thoroughly. I think if there'd been a heated argument, it would've had to be me making it, and I'm not good at arguing, so it just didn't occur."

—Bob Siemann

"We had some pretty heated discussions on some of the damages issues."

—Kathy Spellman

"We had a game called 'Aggravation,' it's similar to Chinese checkers. The rules are that you get so far and somebody else will knock you off the board and you have to start over. Every noon hour and every break we played 'Aggravation' and a lot of times the doors were open, so outside you could hear the dice rolling. But when we deliberated we were very, very serious."

—Pete Crosetto

The foreman of the jury pressed a buzzer three times, to signal that they had reached a verdict.

Betty Burke had been deep in consultation with David Sabih and Harold Hunter. Almost simultaneously with the sound of the buzzer, they arrived at an agreement: if the verdict went against Dr. McReynolds only, Betty would accept $300,-000, no matter what amount the jury awarded. If the verdict was against both McReynolds and Spindle, but the award was under $300,000, she would get $300,000. If the award was over $300,000 but under $600,000, she would get the total amount of the award. If the award was more than $600,000, she agreed to accept $600,000 plus one half of the excess over $600,000.

The jury filed out. The foreman, Don Gilbert, handed the verdict to the clerk, and the clerk read it aloud:

"We, the jury, find for the plaintiff, in the amount of $404,000." The verdict was eleven to one. Only Bob Siemann voted for the defense.

By prior arrangement, Betty's medical bills were paid, and the remainder was split between Betty and her lawyers, 50–50. Betty's share was $182,000.

14.

"It was a very, very close case. This was proved by the extreme length of time it took for the deliberations."

—Harold Hunter

"It was easy to agree that there was negligence. But to what *extent* the doctors were responsible—the amount of the settlement—that was our biggest problem. My main concern was not how much she had lost but her life from now on, what's it going to cost her from now on. After all, how do you put a price on something that's—gone? We all agreed none of us would want to be in that condition for any price."

—Emma Oaks

The plaintiff had presented two economists who gave their estimates of the past and future economic losses to Betty Burke. One of them, Dr. Robert Miller, appraised her lost earnings at $166,285; the cost of substitute mother care for her family at $135,630; of housekeeping services at $177,540; her total medical costs at $223,995; her attendant care costs at $378,745. The total "lost economic value" of Betty Burke's life was $1,082,195. Dr. Miller's computations included only economic damage, not compensation for pain or suffering.

"The two things I was afraid of were either that the verdict would go against her, or that we would 'give her the farm' as Hunter called it. Either one would have been as unfair as the other. I had enough experience to know that plaintiffs always ask for much more than they expect to get. There were figures mentioned of a million or a million and a half."

—Pete Crosetto

"Sabih's ultimate demand was in the millions. I felt it incumbent upon me to argue against the damages he urged and against his unrealistic approach. I tried to compute his figures to everyday consumer items—how many homes that would buy mortgage-free, and so on. I argued that the jury's duty was merely to compensate her, not to create an estate for her heirs and survivors. This had a salutary effect in tempering the award."

—Harold Hunter

"Someone would scream for something way up and someone else wanted something a lot lower, and we came up and came down . . ."

—Emma Oaks

A couple of weeks after the trial was over, I went to Hawaii with my girlfriend and our kids. Then her husband and my mother came over and joined us. We chartered a yacht to visit the outer islands, and we had a luau . . .

We were there at Christmas, and I was going to send Gene a telegram from the kids to wish him a Merry Christmas. But before I sent it I got a phone call from him. I said, I was just about to send you a telegram. He said, Don't bother, I'm in the hotel next door.

So he had Christmas dinner with us. He wanted for us to get together and try it again, but I wasn't having any.

So we went out on the yacht, he didn't come with us, and when we got back he'd gone.

"After it was all over we had a party at a restaurant-night club in Norwalk. Sabih reserved a table for thirty people and said we should have whatever we wanted, so we did. And then he paid the bill."

—Pete Crosetto

Betty Burke bought the ranch that she had dreamed, as a child, of owning.

I keep quite busy. I do the books for the ranch; my son Mitch is in the Junior Rodeo Association and I take him and his friends and the horses wherever they have to go.

I have a Citizens' Band radio, I talk to people as far away as Texas. Sometimes the closer ones get together and have coffee klatches. I take care of all my personal needs, cook and clean—of course my Mom tries to keep me from doing too much.

I have a friend, who's a triple amputee from the Vietnam war, who started a recreational ranch for the handicapped about seven miles from here. I'm on the Board of Directors, so I answer mail and help make decisions. So far we've had five or so people stay there and we're hoping to expand. We teach them to ride, and we plan to have pool, a shooting range, miniature golf specially made for people in wheelchairs. They pay if they can afford it.

I'm having a saddle made so I can ride. It's a special kind that won't show I'm handicapped, because I don't want any special favors when I show a horse.

The ranch is doing pretty well, though of course the cattle market right now is the lowest in the history of the United States. It's really a wonderful life. I just hope we can manage.

15.

"You're going for treatment, you know there's always a risk in surgery. It's too bad these things happen. If things improve to the point where they can be avoided or made better, that'll be fine. But in the meantime you just have to accept the risks."

—Bob Siemann

Closing argument of Mr. Shapiro:

"You have heard all the expert witnesses, and I think that you have heard that every one was in substantial agreement that if the dura had been sewn at the time of the first operation there would not have been a spinal fluid leak, no cyst would have formed, no second operation would have been necessary, no arachnoiditis . . ."

The doctor blew it. That was a fact I couldn't change. But I know it is not beyond the realm of possibility that medical miracles can be performed. I've done research, I've found that they are experimenting with transplanting nerves in the lower lumbar. I don't know but that tomorrow, in some land, some scientist may be able to transplant a whole spinal cord.

Right after the last surgery, almost immediately, Spindle came into my room and said, I want you to completely understand something. There is no God going to come down here and perform a miracle. You will never walk again.

I said, I want to tell you something. Don't you tell me that my God can't do anything He wants to. Don't you tell me how to feel about God. Now you get out of here and don't you ever come in this room again.

You know . . . I have nothing wrong with my arms. I have nothing wrong with my top. I think, basically, considering everything that has happened to me, I have got it pretty well together in my head.